ALG
ALGARVE

AMAZING EXPERIENCES | DISCOVERY TOURS | PULL-OUT MAP | Travel with **Insider Tips**

CW01572824

MARCO POLO TOP HIGHLIGHTS

ALBUFEIRA ⭐1
The best beaches in the area. Lots of great cafés, bars and restaurants. And there's even a marina.

➤ p. 87, The Barlavento

LAGOS ⭐2
This is where Henry the Navigator wrote his buccaneering adventure stories. Today its charm comes from the port and the atmospheric old city.

➤ p. 70, The Barlavento

FARO'S VILA-ADENTRO (OLD TOWN) ⭐3
In the middle of the buzzing modern city, Faro's old town – with its cathedral, monastery and web of tiny lanes – feels a bit like a museum.

➤ p. 47, The Sotavento

CULATRA ⭐4
Take the ferry to the traffic-free islands of Culatra and Armona. Far from the bustle of the coast, it is a whole different world out there.

➤ p. 54, The Sotavento

TAVIRA ⭐5
A stunning town of many churches on the Rio Gilão.
📷 *Tip: At the Praia do Barril on the Ilha de Tavira, the huge graveyard of anchors in the sand (photo) makes an epic subject for photos.*

➤ p. 55, The Sotavento

IGREJA DE SÃO LOURENÇO ⭐6
The Baroque church in Almancil has some of the best examples of *azulejo* tiles in the region. The rich, golden decoration provides a clear sense of Portugal's colonial wealth.

➤ p. 50, The Sotavento

LOULÉ 🟥7
The neo-Moorish covered market is the jewel of this pretty inland town. There is also an impressive fortress up on the hill.
📷 *Tip: Come to the market hall first thing in the morning, when the displays of fish are at their most photogenic!*

➤ p. 122, The Hinterland

ARRIFANA 🟥9
The Costa Vicentina's stunning steep cliffs are enough to take anyone's breath away.
📷 *Tip: For great surfing pictures, head to Arrifana beach, where the waves are so high you can see them from the car park.*

➤ p. 108, The West Coast

SERRA DE MONCHIQUE 🟥8
The so-called Garden of the Algarve is the beautiful country-side around the small mountain village of Monchique.
📷 *Tip: Climb onto the rocks at the summit of Fóia for the best views down towards the coast.*

➤ p. 117, The Hinterland

SAGRES 🟥10
Surfers love the waves, foodies love the fish restaurants, and seafaring enthusiasts love the amazing fortress.
📷 *Tip: The stronghold gives you an amazing view along the coast to the lighthouse of Cabo São Vicente.*

➤ p. 100, The West Coast

CONTENTS

CONTENTS

🕑   Plan your visit

€–€€€   Price categories

🍴   Eating/drinking

🛍   Shopping

🍸   Going out

🌴   Top beaches

    Sustainable activities

    Budget activities

    Family activities

    Classic experiences

✅   MARCO POLO Bucket List

(📖 A2) Refers to the removable pull-out map
(0) Located off the map

Loulé's neo-Moorish covered market

BEST OF THE ALGARVE

A natural masterpiece: the Benagil sea cave near Carvoeiro

BEST
GREEN & FAIR

SUSTAINABLE ACTIVITIES

DELICACIES FROM THE SOUTH

You can get delicious wine, even more delicious arbutus (or strawberry tree) fruit liqueur, juicy oranges, spicy chilli peppers and everything else on offer at the region's *covered markets* – all the while supporting local producers.

HEAVENLY HINTERLAND

While the (often quite touristy) coastal resorts are bustling, especially in summer, you will find peace and quiet in the inland villages. Renting a room here helps support the local families, as well as boosting the region's village economy!

ON THE FISHERMEN'S TRAIL

For a completely sustainable (and truly fantastic!) experience, set off on a multi-day hike along the *Rota Vicentina Fishermen's Trail (rota vicentina.com)* (photo), which takes you along the Alentejo and Algarve coasts. Along the way, you can stay in small family-run guesthouses and buy your provisions at the *minimercados* in the villages.

➤ p. 103, p. 109, The West Coast

DUMP THE PLASTIC WATER BOTTLE

When you're in the *Monchique moun-tains* and you see locals filling up water cans from the natural springs, follow their example! Every plastic bottle you don't buy is a win for the environment.

➤ p. 118, p. 122, The Hinterland

BY BUS & RAIL

Although you might not be able to get to every remote beach by public transport, the extensive bus network means you can discover plenty of places without renting a car. There are also some very picturesque local train routes between Lagos and Vila Real de Santo António.

➤ p. 146, Good to know

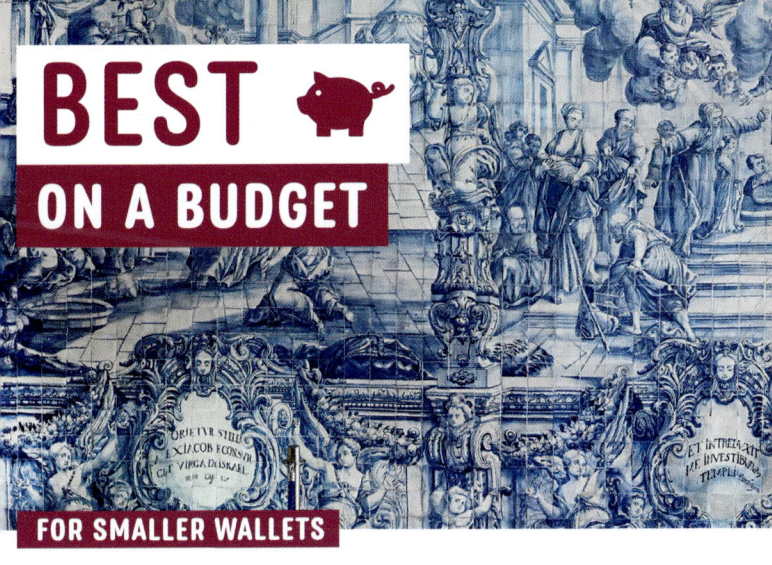

BEST 🐷 ON A BUDGET

FOR SMALLER WALLETS

AFFORDABLE SHOPPING

At *Designer Outlet Algarve* in the retail village between Faro and Loulé (between IKEA and the MAR shopping centre) you can find discounted brand-name clothes.

➤ p. 48, The Sotavento

HILLTOP CASTLE

Perched on a hill, the *castelo* dominates Tavira and its surroundings. There is no admission fee to visit the castle walls, so free your inner child for a few hours and clamber around while enjoying the stunning views.

➤ p. 57, The Sotavento

MUNCIPAL MUSEUMS

The public museums, such as *Museu de Portimão*, are worth a visit and the entry fee is rarely more than 3 euros. There are often inexpensive combination tickets for exhibitions spread across several sites.

➤ p. 79, The Barlavento

BUY TICKETS ONLINE

Top attractions such as *Slide & Splash* waterpark or *Zoomarine* theme park aren't exactly cheap. But you can get discounted tickets if you book online. It's always worth checking the website before any visit.

➤ p. 83, p. 90, The Barlavento

BUY FROM THE GROWERS

Do your bit by supporting local people. Some locals set up stalls in front of their houses and sell home-grown fruit and vegetables.

➤ p. 89, The Barlavento

CHAPEL TEEMING WITH TILES

The *Ermida Nossa Senhora da Conceição* in the historic centre of Loulé is adorned with the most spectacular *azulejos* (photo). You can enjoy this delightful chapel for free.

➤ p. 124, The Hinterland

BEST WITH CHILDREN

FUN FOR YOUNG & OLD

STUDYING STARFISH
The *Centro Ciência Viva do Algarve* is the kind of interactive museum that will get the whole family enthused. You will come out with an understanding of how the *lagunas* on the Ria Formosa were formed … and of what lives in them, from sea cucumbers to hermit crabs and starfish.
➤ p. 44, The Sotavento

A DAY AT THE ZOO
Lemurs, with their long tails and huge eyes, will put a smile on the face of any child. Alongside the primates, the *Zoo de Lagos* has an impressive collection of exotic animals and birds, as well as native sheep and goats and a petting zoo.
➤ p. 76, The Barlavento

GET WET & GO WILD
The clue is in the name at *Slide & Splash*, a waterpark that shows you just how many ways there are to enter the water (some are seriously fast). Make sure your swimsuit doesn't slip down too easily (you will thank us!) and then jump in.
➤ p. 83, The Barlavento

CANOPY CLIMBING
Carabiner secure? Belt tight? Then tally-ho and up to the treetops you (or your kids) go! The high-rope courses at the *Parque Aventura* in Albufeira have something for kids of all ages – from toddler trails up to courses for the "adventurous" and the "fearless".
➤ p. 90, The Barlavento

BRIBING DONKEYS
You won't get far on a *donkey trek* if you don't have any carrots to bribe your trusty – but often pretty stubborn – steed. So long as you can keep them going, a donkey trek is a treat for all the family and the Costa Vicentina has plenty of great routes to explore.
➤ p. 106, The West Coast

BEST 🚩

CLASSIC EXPERIENCES

ONLY IN THE ALGARVE

SMALL WORKS OF ART

Azulejos, painted ceramic tiles, are Portugal's most beautiful contribution to the art world. Their name and origin date back to the Moors: *az-zulayi* means "small stone". They decorate courtyards, hospitals and churches, such as the *Igreja de São Lourenço* in Almancil.
➤ p. 50, The Sotavento

BEACH PARTY

Summertime is party time in the coastal towns along the Algarve, and things get especially wild on the *Praia da Rocha,* in Portimão.
➤ p. 82, The Barlavento

BLUE BEACHES

Blue flags fluttering in the wind guarantee a clean stretch of Algarve coastline, and the pristine white beaches are great adverts for the system. The showcase beach has to be the *Praia da Falésia* near Albufeira.
➤ p. 90, The Barlavento

POSTCARD PERFECT

Bold, bright boats for fishermen (photo); even the large yachts that you see in every harbour add a splash of colour. The most postcard-worthy harbour is *Porto da Baleeira* in Sagres.
➤ p. 100, The West Coast

SURFERS' HAVEN

Because huge waves generate huge fun, surfers are drawn to the Atlantic coast all year round – conditions here are also good for wind- and kite-surfers. The top spot for surf-watching is *Praia do Amado*.
➤ p. 109, The West Coast

MOUNTAIN FIREWATER

Strawberries on bushes? The fruit of the strawberry tree looks convincingly like a strawberry, but these berries are not to be eaten. Instead they are fermented to produce *medronho*. Try it: the strong spirit tastes delicious.
➤ p. 121, The Hinterland

GET TO KNOW THE ALGARVE

Spring in the Algarve means storks nesting on the rooftops and on the city gate in Faro

DISCOVER THE ALGARVE

Jacaranda trees in bloom below Silves cathedral and castle

Many, many hours of sunshine, clean seawater, heavenly beaches, sheltered coves, rocky cliffs and sand dunes galore. If you search for "holiday" online, you might well find a picture taken in the Algarve. And if relaxing on a beach for two weeks is not for you, there is much more to this region than just its glorious sun and sand.

SUMMERS OF SUNSHINE

In summer the whole of the Algarve buzzes with activity. The warm evenings are accompanied by music emanating from the many bars, and in the villages of the hinterland there is always some kind of festival going on. If you like an action-packed holiday, you'll find plenty to do on the coast, from surfing to kayaking. It may seem too hot for hiking, but in the mountains and on the west coast you will

from 1100 BCE
Phoenician settlers build the first ports on the coast

218 BCE–CE 400
The Iberian Peninsula is under Roman rule

711–1249
The period of Moorish rule

From 1419
Under Prince Henry the Navigator the "Era of Discovery" begins

1450
Algarve becomes part of the Kingdom of Portugal

1580–1640
Portugal becomes a vassal state held by the Spanish

often find a refreshing breeze. And the amusement parks are open every day during the summer, so you can channel your inner child as you ride the water-slides. From May to October you will rarely find anything closed, as the bars and restaurants all make hay while the sun very literally shines. Beware: it can get very busy here, as the Portuguese also love their south coast and, during August, half the country descends on the Algarve for a few days' holiday …

THE CALM MIDWINTER

If you travel outside the school holi-days or decide not to spend all your time swimming and sunbathing, you will experience a whole other side to the Algarve. Things quickly quieten down during the autumn, while in winter some people find it a little too quiet – especially once many of the bars and restaurants have gone into hibernation. This time of year is perfect for golf-ers, as well as hikers, cyclists and people looking for peace and quiet. In winter on the Algarve, temperatures can hover at a wonderful 20°C for weeks on end.

THE COLOURS OF SPRING

But it has to rain sometimes, or there wouldn't be so many stunning fields of flowers in spring and summer. Even during the colder half of the year you can find plenty of flora – from pure white almond blossom to glowing yellow acacia groves and the purple-spotted rock rose; and the usually barren coastal macchia suddenly bursts forth in a vibrant green – not to mention the hills of the hinter-land, which can seem almost desert-like in summer.

1755
Severe earthquake destroys many towns and cities

1910
End of the monarchy. Proclamation of the Republic

1932–74
From the Salazar dictatorship to the "Carnation Revolution"

1986
Portugal joins the European Community

2002
Euro currency introduced

2012–14
Economic crisis: Portugal receives EU bail-out package

2025
The A22 motorway finally returns to being toll free

==The winter also offers superb birdwatching, as so many migratory birds spend the winter here.== During the spring the birds flutter between the rooftops, and from March onwards it is difficult to find an electricity poles that doesn't have a stork's nest on top of it.

SURPRISING DIVERSITY

Whatever time of year you visit the Algarve, it's worth exploring all the different regions in the province and their extraordinary diversity. The best way to do this is to rent a car. Often just a few kilometres separate the buzzing coastal towns from secluded mountain villages; the tranquil coves on the rocky coast are less than an hour away from the rough and untamed west coast; and, from the beautiful towns of the eastern Algarve, it's just a short boat trip across the lagoons of the Ria Formosa to the almost endless sandy beaches of the barrier islands.

ALL WELL IN PARADISE?

The isolated mountain villages may seem picturesque but rural exodus is a serious problem – especially when it's only the older people who stay behind. The fishing industry is no longer able to support the population and forest fires have left their mark, as have the crises (financial, Covid-19, inflation) of recent years, and housing has become unaffordable for locals. Even though tourism may be booming once again, it is fundamentally a seasonal industry. A lot of mistakes have been made in the tourism business too, as evidenced by numerous unfinished buildings and overly developed parts of the coast. It remains to be seen whether oil drilling off the coast will be a success or not. But Algarvios display an irrepressible Mediterranean nonchalance and simply make the best out of the situation.

DEEP SOUTH OR FAR WEST?

But what exactly is the homeland of the Algarvios? It's the southernmost tip of Portugal, stretching like an elongated rectangle from the Spanish border in the east to the Atlantic coast in the west. The 150km-long southern coastline is naturally divided into two halves: in the west, the dramatic, rocky coast of the Barlavento; and in the east, the Sotavento, characterised by enormous beaches with dunes and lagoons. To the north of this lies a landscape of hills and mountains that extends around 50km to the border with the neighbouring province of Alentejo. The official name for the Algarve is the rather uninspiring *Distrito de Faro* – it is just one of 17 administrative districts in Portugal, and is simply named after its regional capital. However, the Moors who ruled over the region from the eighth until the 13th century came up with a more beautiful-sounding name: *Al-Gharb*, meaning "the West", as this was the westernmost part of their Caliphate on the Iberian Peninsula. They were very reluctant to submit to the Christian Reconquista; you may well find yourself as reluctant to leave as they were all those centuries ago.

AT A GLANCE

467,340
population

Bristol 472,400 (2021)

200km
Coastline

Pembrokeshire coastline: 299km

4,997km²
Total area

Kent: 3,736km²

HIGHEST MOUNTAIN: FÓIA
902m

WARMEST & MOST POPULAR MONTH
AUGUST 28°C

HOURS OF SUN PER YEAR
3,000

LONDON: 1,410

AREA WITH THE MOST EXPENSIVE HOTELS

Quinta do Lago (approx. 800 euros for a double room in August in the Hotel Conrad Algarve)

GOLF

36 golf courses
Scotland: 550

BRITS' PARTY AREA
"The Strip" (Av. Dr Francisco Sá Carneiro, Albufeira)

FRUIT NEEDED TO MAKE 1 LITRE OF _MEDRONHO_: 8KG

UNDERSTAND THE ALGARVE

THE MOUNTAINS ARE CALLING

For many years, it was the seaside that beckoned, as native Algarvios flooded from the hinterland into the rapidly expanding coastal towns in pursuit of promising job opportunities in the booming tourism industry. Life on the coast seemed more appealing than working in the region's back-breaking traditional agricultural industry; only the elderly were left behind in their villages, and some areas are now virtually deserted. Attempts, such as the Via Algarviana long-distance hiking trail, have been made to attract tourists to these remote regions. However, they have – as yet – only achieved modest success in bringing life back to the villages. And yet these are remarkable places, situated within a stunning hilly landscape – sometimes barren, sometimes covered in cork oak forests, and criss-crossed with fantastic hiking trails. Make sure you head up into the Serra do Caldeirão or the Serra de Monchique for a walk, and afterwards pop into one of the remaining traditional village taverns for a glass of medronho with the locals. You won't regret it.

INSIDER TIP
Get in the spirit!

CORK CRAZE

Every bottle of Portuguese wine is sealed with real cork, and the craze for this natural, waterproof product does not stop there. Walk into a souvenir shop and you will encounter cork products of every imaginable kind, from postcards to finely carved sculptures. To discover why there is so much interest in this ancient natural material, which is both waterproof and fireproof, take a trip into the Serra de Monchique. Here, beautiful ancient trees shed one layer of cork cells every nine years. The cork farmers keep track of when each tree is due a harvest by writing the year of the last harvest on the trunk. This is no way to make a quick buck … nonetheless the Portuguese have turned cork into one of their most important exports and are the world's biggest producer. If you are interested in learning how to turn bark into bottle stoppers, the processing plant in São Brás de Alportel offers guided tours.

GLEAMING WALLS

Tilers in Portugal during the 18th and 19th centuries must have been exhausted – there is hardly a church in the whole country that isn't decorated with azulejos … Particularly splendid examples from this period include the Igreja de São Lourenço, on the edge of Almancil, and the Igreja de Santo António, in Lagos. However, the tradition is much older, and was originally introduced by the Moors, who gave these tiles their name: al-zulij, or "small polished stone". The tiles are frequently painted in blue and white

Here the miracle material has already been harvested: cork oak in the Serra de Monchique

and are more than just attractive decorative objects – they also serve as a heat- and weather-resistant wall lining.

SMALL FRY

You can find fresh fish on the menu in every restaurant, which makes sense – we are on the coast here, after all. But is all this fish really caught locally? The bream and sea bass generally come from fish farms, the *bacalhau* (dried cod) is imported from Norway, and the only relics of the golden age of tuna fishing are the former factories (now converted into tourist attractions), like those in Quatro Águas or on the Praia do Barril in Tavira. The formerly widespread fish-canning industry has also been reduced to just two canneries. However, if you pay a visit to the fishing ports of Olhão, Portimão, Quarteira,

Alvor or Sagres, you will see that there are still fresh fish to be caught – as well as men working hard to catch them. This is particularly the case in summer, which is sardine season. Both the ports and the indoor fish markets paint a vivid picture of this industry, which was the region's most important right up until the 20th century. Incidentally, the bright colours of the fishing boats were primarily for safety – to make them more visible in the fog – rather than aesthetics.

LIVING LAGOON

You probably caught an initial glimpse of the enormous Ria Formosa – with its mud flats, channels, sandbanks, rows of dunes and salt marshes – from your plane on the way into Faro airport, as the flight path cuts directly across this 170km² nature park. The many birds that inhabit this protected area have grown accustomed to their huge metal counterparts flying overhead and seem unfazed by them. The Ria Formosa is a truly remarkable natural feature. This lagoon landscape measuring around 60km in length, is one of the biggest and most beautiful in Europe. The area is separated from the

well worth taking a guided boat tour through the *ria*, as you will see a whole host of unusual plants and animals (especially birds). The nature park centre *Quinta de Marim* in Olhão also offers plenty of information about the origins of the *ria* and the many living creatures that can be found there, with a well-designed nature trail leading across the premises.

Is it a church tower? Is it a minaret? No, it's a typical Algarvian chimney!

sea by enormous sandbanks, and at high tide it transforms into an intricate network of rivulets, channels and marshes. The sandbanks themselves are lined with seemingly endless idyllic beaches, a few of which are inhabited – generally by cockle-pickers and fishermen. Some are accessible via a causeway, while others can only be reached by boat. It is

ORNATE CHIMNEYS

It is hardly surprising that these distinctive chimneys have become an emblem of sorts for the Algarve. Some are round, others oblong. It doesn't matter whether the house is old or new – chimneys give houses in the Algarve character. Historians suspect they were originally camouflaged minarets, from the time when the region was claimed back from the Moors and Christianity was enforced with a vengeance.

MANUEL THE MAGNIFICENT

King Manuel I was known as "the Fortunate", as during his reign Portugal experienced the high point of its global fame and wealth thanks to the voyages of exploration led by Vasco da Gama and other seafarers. Portugal became a central figure in the global spice trade, and then faced the question of what to do with its new-found wealth. Like nouveau riche people everywhere, Manuel built. He commissioned magnificent monasteries, churches, towers and palaces throughout the country, all of which were covered in delicate decorative maritime elements. Although many buildings from this period were destroyed by the huge earthquake in 1755, it is still possible to find architectural relics from Portugal's golden age. These include the "Manueline" windows and doorways on the village churches in Monchique, Luz de Tavira and Alvor, which are covered in ornaments including exotic plants, corals and mooring ropes. The style is truly unique to Portugal.

MOORISH REMNANTS

Citrus, carob and almond trees; irrigation systems; profitable fishing methods; flourishing global trade; religious tolerance and plenty of culture … The Moors brought a great deal to the region during their rule, which began in 711 and lasted until the middle of the 13th century.

TRUE OR FALSE?

SEA AS WARM AS A JACUZZI?

False! If you're heading to the south of Portugal, you probably expect sea temperatures which you could comfortably bathe in. Unfortuna-tely, you are set to be disappointed. This is the Atlantic and it lacks the balmy warmth of the Med. Even in August the water rarely gets much above 20°C. Compared to Croatia, for example, where water temperature regularly hits 27°C, this can feel pretty icy. However, once you've experienced the extreme heat of an Algarve summer, you are likely to see the refreshing cold as a blessing.

A FISHY PEOPLE?

True! Sardines in the summer, mussels in every month with an "r" in it, and bass, cod, octopus and tuna for the rest of the year. The Algarvios eat seafood like it's going out of fashion (and it kind of is). This is not a place where one says "I don't like fish", and you won't find a menu at a restaurant or local festival without at least a couple of seafood options. It's part of the local culture and quite a few people here still make their living from the sea. Top tip: if you are tempted by more than one fishy option in a restaurant, order the *cataplana*, a selection of dishes which is meant to show off the chef's skills.

However, aside from numerous place names (including all those beginning with "Al" or "Gua"), some all-too-perfectly restored fortresses, such as the one in Silves, and a few archaeological relics, not much is left of their legacy today. The Reconquista (the re-conquest of Iberia) took place in the depths of the Middle Ages, and the Christian knights showed little mercy when it came to the architectural legacy of the Muslim Almohad dynasty. All the region's mosques were replaced with churches in this period, and much of what was left was destroyed in the 1755 earthquake. Many of the existing remnants can be found in the picturesque town of Mértola in Alentejo.

ALL MANNER OF MUSIC

During the summer, live music pumps out of every kind of nightlife establishment. Whether you are into hard rock or chilled-out jazz, you will find a place to fill a few melodious hours at pretty much any time of day or night; for example, the *Café Inglês* (see p. 115) in Silves hosts jazz sessions on Sunday afternoons. Nowadays, several towns also stage fantastic music festivals in their historic centres, with highlights including the annual world music *Festival MED* at the end of June in Loulé and the *Festival F* at the beginning of September in Faro.

And then of course, there is *fado* – the traditional Portuguese song genre that expresses a sense of mournful yearning. Originating from the poor quarters of Lisbon during the 19th century, it is traditionally accompanied by the distinctively bulbous *guitarra portuguesa* and a classical guitar, and is now classed by UNESCO as an Intangible Cultural Heritage. The genre is not actually typical of the Algarve, but can still be heard in many places – for example, at the cultural association *Fado com História,* in Tavira.

SALT MOUNTAINS

You will see the gleaming white mountains of salt dotted along the Ria Formosa or in Castro Marim. And you will also find it on sale as a typical Algarve souvenir at any market. But how exactly is salt "harvested"? During the summer, huge basins in the salt marshes are flooded with seawater. As the water evaporates, the salt concentration gradually increases. When the water is channelled into smaller pans, the crystallisation process begins, and the resulting salt is harvested by hand using wooden rakes. At first, this takes the form of valuable *flor de sal*, a particularly fine salt that forms every day on the surface of the brine; but after two weeks the rest of the salt is collected. This is an ancient tradition which has not changed much since the Romans used Algarve salt to preserve their fish 2,000 years ago.

TIMES OF CRISIS

Large tax increases, funds from the EU rescue package, severe welfare cutbacks, Covid-19 and inflation – Portugal went through hard times in the previous decade, the consequences of which are still being felt. Living standards dropped to a low point and the Portuguese were forced to survive on modest means. Due to a lack of investors, new buildings in the Algarve transformed overnight into ruins while other properties remained empty, waiting for prospective buyers. Nonetheless, property prices have boomed since the crisis, and native Algarvios have found it extremely tough to find places to live. The idea of secure employment and a decent wage is still a pipe dream for many people in the region, and often alternative income streams have to be found. Mind you, the Portuguese have a long history of finding a way to get through even the toughest of times.

WINE TASTING

Life isn't easy for the Algarvian wine industry, as it stands in the shadow of Portugal's major wine regions such as Douro, Dão and Alentejo. However, a few wineries are gradually making a name for themselves, and some have even won major awards. You need only visit one of these *quintas* for a tasting to realise how richly deserved their new-found recognition is. The citrus-coloured white wines are soft and fruity; the rosés come with a raspberry aroma; and the reds are full bodied and characterful. The grapes thrive in the sunny maritime climate and the native *terroir*, particularly in the area around Lagoa; but it takes a lot of hard work to produce a good wine. In the past, the wines here were made almost exclusively by cooperatives, and the quality was middling. Now, increasing numbers of small but highly motivated producers are working with dedication and passion and, lo and behold, they have come up with some superb wines.

The methods for gathering salt at Castro Marim haven't changed since Roman times

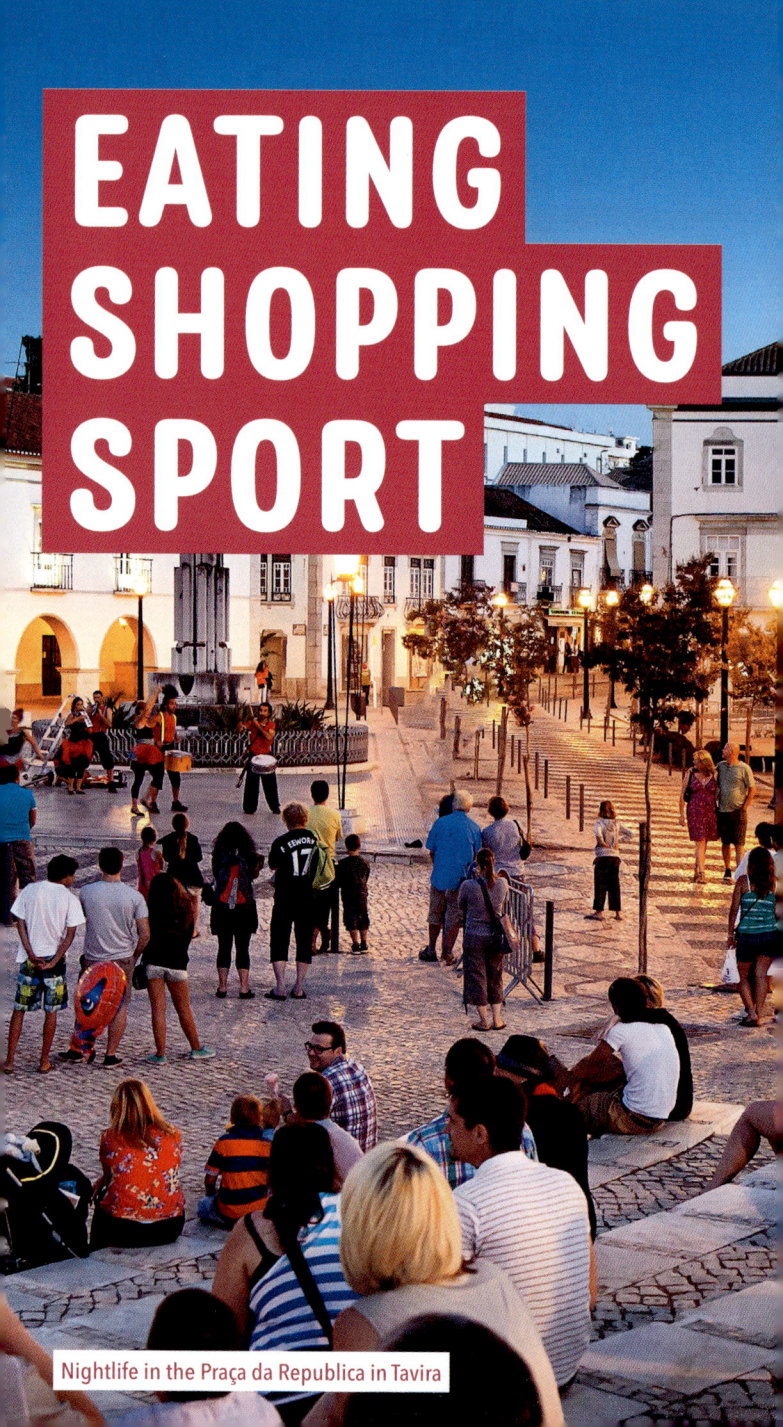

EATING
SHOPPING
SPORT

Nightlife in the Praça da Republica in Tavira

EATING & DRINKING

Be it fried, grilled, salted or in kebabs, seafood dominates the Algarve's cuisine.

THE JOY OF EATING

Eating in Portugal is never about just replenishing your energy stocks. Food is celebrated here for its ability to bring friends and families together. At home you may well dash out of the office for a sandwich or force down a soggy salad in the work kitchen, but these modes of eating have no place in the Algarve. The tiny number of fast-food restaurants or chain coffee shops is a reminder that culinary culture here is different; eating takes time and, once you adapt, it is a wonderful thing that it does.

INTERNATIONAL & REGIONAL

A number of restaurants in the region serve French, Italian, Indian or Chinese cuisine. Sometimes you can't beat a decent pizza no matter where in the world you are. For the most part though, the restaurants found in the Algarve serve local dishes, just as they do in the rest of Portugal, with a heavy focus on seafood and meat. The restaurant business is never easy and not every establishment can keep its head above water, especially if they can only earn money during the summer months. There is also a staggering VAT of up to 23 per cent on food and drink in Portugal. Don't be too surprised if any of the places we recommend here no longer exist by the time of your visit (but don't panic, there will be plenty of other great places).

ON A BUDGET

In general, eating out is extremely affordable in Portugal. This obviously does not apply to chic fine-dining restaurants but is true for most simple *tascas*. Some offer a reasonably priced

Essential flavours of the Algarve: *caldeirada* (left) and a glass of *medronho* (right).

three-course set menu for between 10 and 15 euros, which often includes a drink and an espresso. Ordering a restaurant's daily special – *prato do dia* – normally guarantees you speedy service and the freshest ingredients. If you are not ravenous (Portuguese portions can be enormous), you can often order a half portion – *meia dose* – which in reality equates to 70% of a normal portion.

"NOTHING WITH EYES"
It is not too long ago that only very few chefs in the Algarve could understand why anyone would voluntarily refuse to eat meat or fish. Even today it is not unusual to get fish if you ask for a vegetarian option. But times are slowly changing and thankfully it is increasingly common to see a couple of vegetarian dishes on a menu. For a pretty comprehensive list of veggie and vegan restaurants, go to *happy cow.net*.

THE TASTE OF THE SEA
But seafood remains the all-time favourite choice. In the Algarve you can eat fish specialities for 15 euros which would cost you two or three times that in the UK. Most fish is served grilled with boiled potatoes and a hunk of lemon – simple but delicious. If you fancy trying something a bit more adventurous, go for a *cataplana*, one of the Algarve's most traditional dishes and presented in a copper pot (which bears more than a passing resemblance to a UFO). In the pot is a rich mixture of different types of fish (and very often mussels too).

MUSSEL TRAINING
Talking of mussels, the area around the Ria Formosa is responsible for

almost the entire country's shellfish harvest. From *berbigões* (cockles) to *mexilhões* (mussels) and from *lingueirões* (razor clams) to *ostras* (oysters), this area is a shellfish paradise. *Perceves* (goose barnacles) may look like chicken feet but they taste amazing with a cool beer. Due to the constant battering by the waves and water, harvesting them is very risky, which explains the high prices. In general, shellfish is frequently served as an *entrada* (starter).

NO BREAD – NO MEAL

Before you order soup or some other starter, you will typically be offered a *couvert*, which consists of bread, butter, olives and sometimes a carrot salad with a tasty dressing. Feel free to refuse it if you don't feel very hungry as you do have to pay for it. However, for Portuguese people bread is an integral part of every meal, and refusing the bread may raise a few baffled glances from your fellow diners. With good reason too: dunked in soup or used to soak up the cooking juice from mussels or a delicious sauce, it will more than earn its modest keep on your table if you give it a chance.

SWEET DELIGHTS

Desserts in the Algarve will also have you reaching for the nearest possible superlative. A *pudim flan* is delicate and delicious enough but most places also offer a *doce da casa* (home-made dessert) to tempt you. These tantalising delicacies are often made from mixing meringues and almonds with figs, citrus fruits and cream.

SÁUDE!

Most restaurants serve *vinho da casa* (house wines), which are often from Alentejo and normally represent excellent value. However, it is still worth taking a look at the wine list. A well-chilled *vinho verde* (white wine) is the perfect accompaniment to fish dishes. Whites from the Minho region in Portugal's north are young, light and very fresh. As such they are a world away from some of the reds from the Dão or Douro regions, which (while often fantastic) are decidedly heavier. There is also a growing number of decent Algarvian wines. Port comes exclusively from the Douro region but can act as the perfect introduction or conclusion to any meal.

A NIGHTCAP?

Need a digestif after a heavy meal? With either a *medronho* – a brandy made from the strawberry tree – or a *bagaço* (pomace brandy) you have the choice of excellent local options. After that, you can take the edge off the alcohol with a cup of coffee (*bica*). Alternatively, if you have no fear of a hangover, you can order a *bica com cheirinho* (coffee with "firewater"). At this point it really will be time to get out of the restaurant. *"A conta, se faz favor"* will get you to the business end of the evening, as will making the international sign for "The bill, please". In Portugal, it is unusual for there to be complicated negotiations about who ate what. Either one person pays for the whole table or you split evenly so you can make a quick exit! Don't forget to leave a tip (around 10%) on the table.

Today's Specials

Starters

CENOURAS À ALGARVIA
Carrot salad with garlic and
fresh coriander

SOPA DE PEIXE
Hearty fish soup

SALADA DE POLVO
Octopus salad with onions

Main courses

PEIXE DO DIA
Catch of the day prepared on the grill:
pargo (bream), *espadarte* (swordfish)
or *robalo* (sea bass)

SARDINHAS ASSADAS
Grilled sardines with boiled potatoes
and salad (ideally only in summer)

CALDEIRADA
A traditional seafood stew

FRANGO PIRI-PIRI
Grilled chicken in a spicy sauce
(familiar from the one of the UK's
most popular chain restaurants)

Desserts

DOM RODRIGO
Sweet treat made from almonds,
cinnamon and angel hair (sweet threads
of egg boiled in sugar syrup)

TORTA DE ALFARROBA E MEL
Sweet roll made from carob flour,
honey, almonds and eggs

QUEIJO DE FIGO
Fig and almond cake
(not, in fact, a cheese at all)

Drinks

VINHO REGIONAL
Wine from the Algarve

CERVEJA SAGRES
Beer (which is actually brewed
north of Lisbon, not in Sagres)

MEDRONHO
Digestif made from the fruits of
the strawberry tree

CAFÉ/BICA
Small, strong coffee
(very like an espresso)

SHOPPING

CORKY DESIGN
The bark of the cork oak trees is not only transformed into cork for bottles or floors, but also into beautiful accessories. Created from "cork leather", these include glasses cases, belts, bags, umbrellas, hats, sandals, wallets and more. Waterproof, flexible and fire resistant, cork leather has become a great alternative to animal leather for those who wish to avoid using animal products. And when you run a hand over it, you will discover a velvety softness which elevates it above run-of-the-mill cow hide. It's true: cork is the most common, most beautiful and most practical Portuguese export.

NOT IDEAL FOR PLATE SPINNING
If you think Portuguese pottery is just a lot of ancient tiles, then think again. Near Porches, on the N125, there are several ceramic workshops selling a huge range of products, from beautifully designed plates and bowls to colourful teacups and elegant vases. You can even commission your ceramic item of choice. *Azulejos* are of course available too, as is perhaps the most Portuguese of all pottery … the ceramic sardine!

A UFO FOR YOUR HOUSE
Looking for a bed pan or need some decor for a space-themed party? Then buy yourself your very own *cataplana*: You never know you might even cook with it one day too …

COLOURFUL COCKERELS WHEREVER YOU LOOK
You will see colourfully glazed ceramic cockerels virtually everywhere in the Algarve, even though they're an import from Portugal's north. A pilgrim to Santiago de Compostela was accused of theft and brought in front of a judge who happened to be

Souvenirs worth buying: ceramics (left) and cork leather accessories (right)

eating chicken. The pilgrim pled not guilty and claimed that the cockerel would crow as proof of his innocence. Improbably, the deceased chicken then made a sound ... and a legend was born. The souvenir shop industry has been rubbing its hands ever since.

EXTRA HOT

Are you a fan of spicy food? On the Algarve you can find *piri-piri* (chilli) either dried, as a powder, or in sauces – making it ideal for adding some heat to your food.

The strong *medronho* brandy produced and sold mainly in the mountain villages of the Serra de Monchique can also pack quite a bit of heat. *Melosa* (*medronho* with added honey) offers a sweeter alternative.

SWEET-TOOTHED TASTINESS

You can find sweet and fruity cakes made of figs, almonds and honey, and there are also endless varieties of biscuits made with the same ingredients – as well as carob (*alfarroba*) and sweet potato (*batata doce*) – all of which make great souvenirs. Almost every supermarket will have a shelf dedicated to these delicacies.

SALT & SHAKE

Sea salt and the highly prized *flor de sal* from the Algarve's saltworks are sold in attractive little bags all over the region. The salt is often mixed with all kinds of herbs and spices, from thyme to piri-piri and lemon zest. Salt in Loulé's market is very good value (around 3 euros a bag). Light but local and absolutely delicious, it makes an excellent gift for everyone back home.

INSIDER TIP
Souvenirs which will actually get used!

SPORT & ACTIVITIES

From diving and snorkelling to surfing, kayaking and sailing – the Algarve is an ideal choice for water-sports enthusiasts.

But there are also lots of things to do on dry land: Portugal's south is famous for its golf courses, and its diverse landscape is ideal for hiking, biking or horse riding.

CYCLING

Although the markings on the 214-km east–west *Ecovia* cycle path are a little faded, it is possible to cycle from the *Cabo de São Vicente* to the Spanish border following the coastline along the way. However, several parts of the route require riding on very busy roads. The historic route followed by the *Rota Vicentina (rotavicentina.com)* long-distance trail is suited to any cyclists, while the *Via Algarviana (viaalgarviana.org)* is best attempted by those wanting to recreate Tour de France mountain stages. Unsurprisingly, mountain bikes are a must on the latter route. Guided mountain-bike tours – including from the summit of Mount Fóia down to the coast – are available from *Outdoor Tours (outdoor-tours.com)*. If you prefer to pick your own route you can also hire bikes at *Megasport (megasport-travel.com/en)* in Loulé or *Abilio Bikes (abiliobikes.com)* in Tavira.

HIKING

There is a surprising variety of beautiful hiking routes: you can choose between narrow paths along the rocky coastal cliffs or the Costa Vicentina – primarily via the marked routes of the *Rota Vicentina (rotavicentina.com)* trail – through the laguna landscapes of the Ria Formosa or the Ria de Alvor, or up and down through the hilly hinterland. Everywhere in summer will be very hot, while in the spring the

Gain a different perspective by paddling around the cliffs of Ponta da Piedade

trailside will be an explosion of wild-flowers. You can find excellent guided tours in the west offered by brilliant guides like *Ana Carla Cabrita (tel. 9 25 54 55 15 | walkingsagres.com)* who truly knows every inch of the rugged west coast like the back of her hand. She can identify every flower and rock, and she has a wealth of exciting stories about smugglers and fishermen.

INSIDER TIP
Over hill and dale with Ana

HORSE RIDING

Lusitano horses are a popular choice in the Algarve. Despite being Arab thoroughbreds (famed for their hot-blooded temperament), they are well behaved and easy to control – and also very comfortable to ride. Just about every riding school *(centro hípico)* uses Lusitanos.

Quinta da Saudadek (40 euros for 1½-hr hack | tel. 9 68 05 40 13 | cavalosquintadasaudade.com) at Guia offers guided horse riding around the Lagoa dos Salgados, including to the beach at Praia Grande near Armação de Pêra or through the dunes. The horses and ponies are very tame and suitable for beginners.

The *Horse Shoe Ranch (tel. 2 82 47 13 04 | horseshoeranch.de)* in Mexilhoeira Grande offers riding holidays for all levels (800–960 euros/week), including full board and accommodation in one of four apartments.

KAYAK TRIPS

One of the best water-sport experi-ences on the Algarve – at least when conditions are good – is to paddle along the rugged rocky coast and explore the golden grottoes of the Ponta da Piedade in Lagos. A guided kayak tour lasts around three hours and costs 30 euros at *Outdoor Tours*

Hiking near Barranco do Velho

(*Lagos* | *kayak-lagos.pt), though there* are other providers available.

The canals and lagoons of the Ria Formosa are also ideal for exploring by kayak, and you can see plenty of birdlife on the two-hour guided tour run by *Formosamar (50 euros | Faro marina | formosamar.com).*

PADDLEBOARDING & SURFING

The best place to ride the waves is the west coast – especially the Praia do Amado, the Praia da Arrifana and the area around Sagres. Windsurfers and kitesurfers love the Meia Praia at Lagos, the beaches around Portimão and the Ilha de Faro. Stand-up paddleboarding is very popular, and during the summer you can see people on their boards all along the south coast. Beware: the Atlantic Ocean can be unpredictable, so if you are inexperienced consider taking a course – e.g. at *Algarve Watersports (algarvewatersports.com)* in Lagos.

ROCK CLIMBING

Unlike many areas of southern Spain, the Algarve is not exactly famous among rock climbers; however, there are crags available on the slopes of the flat Rocha da Pena as well as on the rocky cliffs at Sagres and the Cabo de São Vicente. The climbing scene is still small here, with an informal, low-key atmosphere.

Guided climbing tours and courses for all levels are available from *Climbing Algarve (from 60 euros/ 2 pers. | climbingalgarve.pt);* equipment is included.

RUNNING

Fancy a holiday half marathon? Almost every town organises one, and there are also a large number of trail-running events each year. Upcoming events are listed on the *Associação do Atletismo do Algarve website: crono.aaalgarve.org.*

SAILING

The wind conditions at Europe's southwestern edge make it an ideal place for sailing. Rainer Klemm and his experienced team offer a one-hour taster course on a catamaran: *Sailcompany (75 euros | tel. 9 10 39 37 00 | sailcompany.com).* This company based on the Meia Praia at Lagos is a member of the Association of Windsurfing and Water Sports Schools (VDWS), which means that the sailing certificates you can obtain here are recognised internationally. There is also a private hour-long taster course costing 50 euros (for two people) that will take you along the Lagos coastline with its many grottoes.

SCUBA DIVING

The diversity of fish species – particularly in Sagres – is huge and visibility is generally very good unless you catch an unfavourable current. The water can be very cold, so thick wetsuits are advisable. To learn the basics with experienced instructors, the team at *Blue Ocean Divers (blue-ocean-divers.eu)* offer courses in English, German and Portuguese.

Lagos also offers lovely diving spots; you can either start directly from land, or you can head out to the spectacular Sagres rocks, or (for very experienced divers) the wrecks at *Ocean Revival Park* in Portimão.

All diving schools offer beginners' courses for those wanting to dip their toe (and quite a lot more besides) into the world of scuba diving. If you enjoy these taster sessions, you can carry on and get your PADI certificate, allowing you in the future to dive without an instructor being present. It's a ticket to a whole new underwater world!

Surf into the sunset

HOLIDAY PLANNER

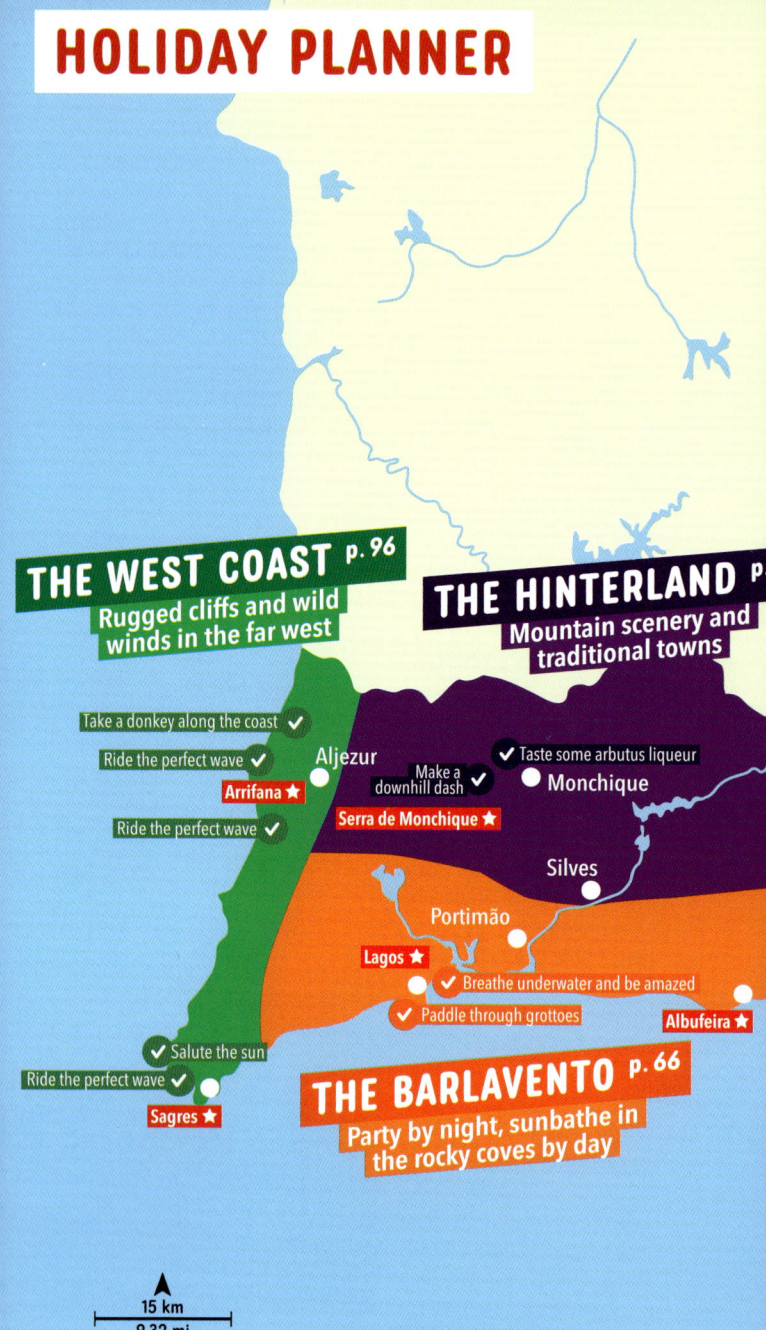

THE WEST COAST p. 96
Rugged cliffs and wild winds in the far west

THE HINTERLAND p.
Mountain scenery and traditional towns

Take a donkey along the coast ✔

Ride the perfect wave ✔

Arrifana ★

Aljezur

Ride the perfect wave ✔

Make a downhill dash ✔

✔ Taste some arbutus liqueur

Monchique

Serra de Monchique ★

Silves

Portimão

Lagos ★

✔ Breathe underwater and be amazed

✔ Paddle through grottoes

Albufeira ★

✔ Salute the sun

Ride the perfect wave ✔

Sagres ★

THE BARLAVENTO p. 66
Party by night, sunbathe in the rocky coves by day

15 km
9.32 mi

THE SOTAVENTO p. 40

Lagoons, salt flats and vast sandy beaches

Alcoutim

✔ Fly over the border

ESPAÑA

Rio Guadiana

Vila Real de Santo António

Loulé ★

✔ Cork it

Tavira ★

Estói

Igreja de São Lourenço ★

Vila-Adentro (old town) ★

Faro   Olhão

Culatra ★

✔ Swim alone from a deserted beach

O C É A N O

A T L Â N T I C O

Rio Guadiana

✔ Marco Polo Bucket List   Marco Polo Top Highlights ★

THE SOTAVENTO

BEAUTIFUL BEACHES & SCINTILLATING CITIES

What makes the Algarve such a great place to visit is its many contrasts. A little to the west of Faro is the start of the sandy part of the Algarve coast. From here to the Rio Guadiana on the Spanish border there is not a rocky cove to be seen; the high cliffs are replaced by glorious, long sandy beaches, which rarely feel crowded, even in summer.

Many of these beaches are located on the islands of the Ria Formosa conservation area – a set of lagoons whose salt flats, flocks

Sand and sea in the Ria Formosa natural park at Tavira

of flamingos and shellfish of every variety make for a stunning landscape and rich culture. Some of the Algarve's most exciting towns and cities were founded hundreds of years ago on the shores of the Ria Formosa. Take some time to explore them; each has its own special character. You can find solitude and wilderness in the hilly hinterland to the east. In fact, if you are looking for peace and quiet on your holiday, then the eastern end of the Algarve is the place to be.

THE SOTAVENTO

MARCO POLO HIGHLIGHTS

★ **FARO'S VILA-ADENTRO (OLD TOWN)**
Faro's historical old town – a medieval island in the modern world ➤ p. 47

★ **IGREJA DE SÃO LOURENÇO**
Dream in blue and white: Baroque chapel with *azulejo* walls ➤ p. 50

★ **MILREU**
Traces of Ancient Rome, with beautiful mosaics ➤ p. 51

★ **OLHÃO**
A jolly port with a lively waterfront promenade and a thing for cuboid houses ➤ p. 51

★ **CULATRA**
A short ferry trip and you can explore this offshore island and its neighbour, Armona ➤ p. 54

★ **TAVIRA**
A picturesque riverside town with a church on every corner ➤ p. 55

★ **ALCOUTIM**
A sleepy fortress town with a zipline across the Spanish border ➤ p. 65

Most tourists rent a car to discover the Algarve and all its beaches and attractions. But the area does have a good bus network, particularly around Faro and between the bigger cities.

Don't visit Olhão on Sunday because the iconic covered market will be closed. Saturday morning is the liveliest time.

BEJA
Giões

FARO
PORTUGAL
397

95 km, 1 hr

Alportel

2

Loulé

São Brás de Alportel

Santa Catarina da Fonte do Bispo

270

A22

Santa Bárbara de Nexe

Santo Estêvão

Vale Formoso

Almancil 2

Milreu ★ 3 3 Estói

6 Moncarapacho

Luz de Tavira

Igreja de São Lourenço ★

IC4

Pechão

Quelfes

5 Fuseta

Conceição

Olhão ★ p. 51

Quinta do Lago

125

3 km, 30 mins

Armona

Faro p. 44

Vila-Adentro (old town) ★

4 Culatra ★

4 km
2.49 mi

Ilha Deserta (Ilha da Barreta) 1
2 ✓

Alcaria Alta Pereiro · IC27 · ESPAÑA · **13** Alcoutim ★ **10** ✓

You will find a completely different, unspoiled, rural Algarve along the border river, Rio Guadiana, best explored via a day's boat trip to Alcoutim.

Odeleite · San Silvestre de Guzmán

If you're looking for the perfect urban accommodation in Sotavento, you have the choice of Faro (busier) or Tavira (calmer), but of course you have a choice of accommodation options all along the coast.

IC27 · Azinhal

Why not take a little detour to Andalusia? You can drive from Vila Real de Santo António to Seville in an hour and a half!

53km, 1¼ hrs · A49

12 Reserva Natural do Sapal de Castro Marim · Ayamonte

Castro Marim **11** · Isla Cristina

Vila Real de Santo António p. 61

A22 · Monte Gordo · Isla Canela

Vila Nova de Cacela · Altura · **Praia Verde**

10 Cacela Velha

Conceição

Tavira ★ · p. 55

9 Praia de Cabanas · Cabanas de Tavira

8 Ilha de Tavira

7 Santa Luzia

Praia do Barril

Many of the beaches on the dune islands off Faro, Olhão and Tavira can only be reached by boat, but these run very frequently in the summer.

It's worth taking the train between Faro and Vila Real de Santo António, where the line runs parallel to the coast and offers amazing views.

O C E A N O
A T L Â N T I C O

MARCO POLO BUCKET LIST

2 ✓ Swim alone from a deserted beach

The *Ilha Deserta* has miles of sand, just for you ➤ p. 50

10 ✓ Fly over the border

Zipline across the Guadiana border river from Spain to Alcoutim ➤ p. 65, p. 137

FARO

(📖 M7–8) **If the only place you visit in Faro is its airport, you are missing out. It's worth spending some time in the Algarve's capital to visit its charming old town, *Vila-Adentro*. But there is much more to this small city than a few pretty, old buildings.**

Faro (pop. 67,650) is a breath of fresh air – it's just an ordinary city, with a university, shopping precincts, industrial estates and, above all, lots of Portuguese people who live, study, shop and work here. You might find lots of tourists in the old town, but the atmosphere is different to that of other towns in the Algarve, partly thanks to the alternative student bar scene. Faro also has plenty of culture on offer, with a theatre, museums, churches and a fascinating history.

The port city was called Ossonoba by the Romans, while the Moors knew it as Harúm. Faro was the last fortress held by the Moors in Portugal before King Alfonso III "reconquered" it in 1249. After the earthquake in 1755 destroyed large parts of Lagos, the Algarve's regional administration was moved from there to Faro, at which point the city began to develop into the country's southern capital.

SIGHTSEEING

CENTRO CIÊNCIA VIVA DO ALGARVE 🎎

In 1910, when the first electric street-lights lit up Faro's narrow streets, a small power station was built on the edge of the Ria Formosa. Today, it has been transformed into an interactive science museum which will help you to understand how the Ria Formosa was formed and will introduce you to many of the flora and fauna, such as sea cucumbers and hermit crabs, that populate it today. However, its past life as a power station has not been completely erased. In the garden, a small wind and tidal power station creates green energy. Do not miss the chance to come in the hours of darkness (registration is necessary). Once the sun goes down, the museum sets up a telescope in the garden which provides glorious views of the stars over the Algarve. *Tue–Sun 10am–1pm and 2–6pm | admission 5 euros (children 3 euros) | Rua Comandante Francisco Manuel | ccvalg.pt | ⊙ 1½ hrs*

INSIDER TIP Stargaze

IGREJA DE SÃO FRANCISCO

Perhaps due to its unremarkable exterior, barely anyone visits this 17th-century monastic church. However, there are few better examples of why not to judge a building by its cover than this little gem. The interior positively drips with stunning *azulejos* and golden woodcuts. Don't just peek in either, the further inside you go, the more colourful it becomes. *Mon–Fri from 9.30am | admission 2 euros | Largo de São Francisco 51*

IGREJA NOSSA SENHORA DO CARMO

The ossuary chapel *(Capela dos Ossos)*, built in 1816 in the garden of the Carmelite church, displays this rather ominous warning above its entrance: "Take heed for you too will end up like this one day". The skulls and bones come from over 1,200 monks who belonged to the order. The church itself is decorated much more cheerfully in a Baroque style. Built in the 18th century, it is lavishly decorated with *talha dourada*, or gilded woodcarvings. *Mon–Fri 9am–1pm and 3–5pm (summer until 6pm), Sat 9am–1pm | admission 2 euros | Largo do Carmo | ⊙ 30 mins*

JARDIM DA ALAMEDA JOÃO DE DEUS

Boisterous peacocks parade around among huge centuries-old trees while parents drink coffee at the *quiosque* and their children charge around the

Take in the view from Faro cathedral's bell tower

playground. Faro's largest city park is not only grand in scale, at its southeastern end there is an imposing former slaughterhouse dating from 1896 decorated with stunning neo-Moorish arches. Fortunately, it's a more peaceful place today, as this bright orange building was converted into the city library in 2001. Shhh .... *Park daily 7.30am–8.30pm (winter until 6pm) | Rua da Polícia da Segurança Pública*

INSIDER TIP
A building that belongs in the Arabian Nights

MUSEU MUNICIPAL

It is worth visiting the city museum for the stunning Renaissance building alone – the 16th-century *Convento de Nossa Senhora da Assunção*, with its two-storey cloister and beautiful garden. But don't forget to check out the exhibitions too, which range from fascinating Roman, Visigoth and Moorish artefacts to a gallery filled with works by local Renaissance and Baroque artists. *Tue–Fri 10am–6pm, Sat/Sun 10.30am–5pm | admission 2 euros,* 🐾 *free Sun until 2pm | Praça Alfonso III 14 | FB: museumunicipalde faro |* ⏱ *1½ hrs*

SÉ

Cameras at the ready! With its elongated, whitewashed bishop's palace (the *Paço Episcopal*), its orange trees and especially the cathedral, the Largo da Sé forms a harmonious and highly photogenic ensemble in the heart of the old town. This site was the location

A bit gruesome: Capela dos Ossos in the Igreja Nossa Senhora do Carmo

of the forum during Roman times; later on, the Visigoths founded a Christian church here before the Moors came and converted it into a mosque. After the Reconquista, construction of a new Christian place of worship was begun on top of these ruins in 1251, but the form of the church was modified in response to an attack by pirates and the 1755 earthquake. Today, it features an exciting mix of styles, from the Gothic bell tower (from the top there are amazing views over the old town and the Ria Formosa) to the lavishly painted Baroque organ installed by the German organ builder Arp Schnitger in 1716. There is a *museum containing sacred art* within the Sé, and you can also visit a small bone chapel in the inner courtyard. *Mon–Fri 10am–7.30pm (winter 10am–6pm), Sat 9.30am–4pm (July/Aug 9.30am–7.30pm) | admission 5 euros*

INSIDER TIP
Far-reaching views over Faro

VILA-ADENTRO (OLD TOWN) ★

Faro's historic centre is supremely picturesque, and its pretty, cobbled streets, the beautiful cathedral precinct of the Largo da Sé and the well-preserved city walls more than make up for the many less attractive parts of town. The *Cidade Velha* is accessed through one of the city gates, the grandest of which is the 18th-century *Arco da Vila* by the *Jardim Manuel Bivar*. The statue above the arch is of the city's patron saint Thomas Aquinas. In spring storks take up residence here by building nests in the

bell tower. Parts of the *Arco do Repouso* (Gate of Rest) date back to the 13th century – this is also where Alfonso III is reputed to have recovered after his battle against the Moors. The conquest of the city is depicted on *azulejo* tiles next to the city gate. The 17th-century *Arco da Porta Nova* leads onto a small promenade that runs parallel to the railway and the Ria Formosa behind it.

EATING & DRINKING

A VENDA

You will notice right away that this small and friendly tapas bar is run by young, throughly dedicated people, even though the decor and the crockery are more reminiscent of your grandma's front room. The dishes are quirky, creative, fresh and well seasoned, and this place is also a paradise for vegetarians. *Closed Sun and Mon lunchtimes | Rua do Compromisso 60 | tel. 2 89 82 55 00 | FB: avendafaro | €*

OUTRO LADO

At the "other side", you will find colourful and exquisite vegan delicacies (which somehow manage to be typically Portuguese). There is such a warm, cosy atmosphere that you'll want to move in! *Closed Sun/Mon and lunchtime | Travessa da Madalena 6 | tel. 9 11 00 03 59 | FB: restoutrolado | €€*

PIGS & COWS

This young, stylish spot offers superb world food (not limited to pork and beef) in a brilliantly designed space. The dishes change regularly according to what is in season and the chef's mood, but often with an Asian twist. You're sure to experience an absolute feast for the eyes and palate. *Closed Mon, Wed and lunchtime | Rua Batista Lopes 57 | tel. 9 66 09 68 50 | pigs andcowsalgarve.com | €€*

TABERNA ZÉ-ZÉ

Choose from succulent seafood *cataplanas* (you have to try the razor clams!), hearty *feijoada* stews with all kinds of seafood, or (if you're only a little bit peckish) delicate tapas – all paired with a suitable wine. Here you can find the best seafood soul food with a friendly atmosphere to go with it. Considering the amazing food on offer, the prices are absolutely fair. Make sure you book in advance. *Closed Sun and lunchtime | Travessa do Alportel 15 | tel. 9 38 73 51 67 | FB: tabernazezefaro | €€*

SHOPPING

Faro's pedestrian zone on *Rua Dom Francisco Gomes* and the surrounding streets offers everything that shoppers could possibly desire. You can find fruit, vegetables and a supermarket at the *market hall (Largo Dr Francisco Sa Carneiro)*. If you love shopping malls, there are a couple of heavy hitters on the outskirts of Faro: the *Forum Algarve (forumalgarve.net)* is located outside the city centre, while a heady combination of IKEA, 🛒 designer outlet stores *(designeroutletalgarve.com)* and a standard mall *(marshopping. com)* is found on the A22 towards Loulé.

SPORT & ACTIVITIES

It's hard to get bored in Faro with the amazing *Ria Formosa* on your doorstep. A number of providers offer boat tours through the channels of this lagoon landscape – or for an even more impressive introduction to this conservation area, try a guided kayak tour. If you are interested in the birdlife on the Ria then you can find some great birdwatching spots in the area around Ludo, to the west of the airport. For all these activities it is worth using the eco-tourism agency *Formosamar (formosamar.com)*, based at the marina.

INSIDER TIP
Paddle through lagoons and canals

BEACHES

Faro's main beach, the *Praia de Faro* on the Ilha de Faro is 10km long. In the 1970s, a building spree took place here, although most of the illegal houses have been demolished. You can find parking and a number of restaurants close to the access road (which runs past the airport and then over a bridge towards the *ria*); however, parking spaces become very scarce during the summer, when half of Faro's population decamps onto the Ilha. The further west you go from the city, the calmer (and more exclusive) the beaches get. The rich and famous tend to hang out in the area around Gigi's beach bar at the 🌴 *Quinta do Lago*. The sand here may stretch for miles in all directions allowing you to

Bags of atmosphere: evening street scene in Faro's old town

contemplate the infinite possibilities of life, the universe and beyond, but the prices in the bar will bring you back to earth with a crash.

WELLNESS

Magic Spa (pestana.com/uk/magic-spa) in the *Palácio de Estói (see p. 51)* is not the cheapest place but its gorgeous setting and excellent attention to detail mean it can justify its sporty prices. You don't need to be a hotel guest to book a massage or to use the sauna and pool.

NIGHTLIFE

There is no shortage of nightlife in Faro, especially in the streets to the north of the marina where you will find countless bars and pubs. Many offer live music during the evening. At *Baixaria Bar (Tue–Sat 10pm–4am | Travessa de São Pedro 10 | IG: @baixariabarfaro)*, for example, you can dance to world music, hip hop or DJ sets. Fancy a cocktail? *Columbus Bar (Sun–Thu noon–2am. Fri/Sat noon–4am | Praça Dom Francisco Gomes 13 | bar columbus.pt)* may look posh from the outside but its prices are fair and the guys behind the bar are veritable magicians of mixology. *O Castelo (daily 9am–4am | Rua do Castelo 11 | ocastelofaro.com)*, by the walls of the old town, has a varied programme of music and cultural events, ranging from fado, tango and jazz to raucous DJ sets. Its lounge-style terrace overlooking the *ria* is a great place for a sundowner, or to enjoy tapas or fresh fish dishes.

INSIDER TIP
Mixology magic

AROUND FARO

1 ILHA DESERTA

7km south of Faro / 15 mins by boat

The boat trip out to the barrier island *Ilha da Barreta* is a unique experience. The island is uninhabited and has no groundwater, which is why it came to be known as the "desert island", or Ilha Deserta. You can dine all year round here at the fantastic and energy self-sufficient beach restaurant *Estaminé (ilhadeserta.com | €€€)*. Booking is essential). Afterwards, there are 7km of empty beach waiting for you, or you can take a stroll through the dunes along the 2km wooden walkway to *Cabo de Santa Maria*, with its bizarre array of driftwood and signposts. *Ferry 10 euros return | bookings via ilhadeserta.com |* 🗺 *M–N8*

INSIDER TIP

Pathway to Portugal's southernmost point

2 ALMANCIL

13km northwest of Faro / 20 mins by car on the IC4/N125

This sprawling town spread out along the busy N125 road doesn't have a huge amount to offer. There are a few cafés and restaurants that are occasionally frequented by wealthy holidaymakers (chiefly golfers) from the neighbouring *Vale do Lobo* and *Quinta do Lago* luxury resorts who are in search of a little authentic Portuguese flair. However, at the eastern end of the town there is a breathtaking church that you shouldn't miss under any circumstances, even if you're not really into church architecture. The small Baroque church ⭐ 🚩 *Igreja de São Lourenço (Mon 3–5pm, Tue–Sat 10am–1pm and 3–5pm | admission 2 euros | Rua da Igreja)* is unique in Portugal: its interior is entirely clad in stunning blue and white *azulejos*. How did a small town like this end up with such a special place of worship? It was financed by the wealthy landowners of the region in order to fulfil a vow made in 1722, which was a particularly dry year. The crops were threatening to fail, so prayers were sent up for water. It rained – and in 1730 the church was completed. 🗺 *L7*

3 ESTÓI & MILREU

10km north of Faro / 15 mins by car on the N2

The highlight of the delightfully relaxed village of Estói (pop. 3,600)

The tiles in the Igreja de São Lourenço create a stunning blue and white display

(□ N7) is the little Belle Époque palace, the *Palácio de Estói (daily 11am–6pm | admission palace 3 euros, garden free | Rua de São José 13),* which today houses a grand *pousada* (small hotel). The splendid Rococo palace once played host to Napoleon Bonaparte's emissaries when they visited the region, and 🐖 its grand salons and chapel and its beautiful garden are open to non-guests. In the park, make sure you check out the sculpture of Venus housed in a "cave" under the steps – three naked goddesses appear to be emerging from a bath in the small fountain.

One kilometre further south, at ⭐ *Milreu (□ M7),* archaeologists unearthed an incredible discovery at the end of the 19th century: a Roman villa dating from the first century CE, which had been continually expanded until the fourth century and featured its own temple. A few mosaics with fish and dolphin motifs have been preserved, and a visit to the excavation site and museum *(May–Sept Tue–Sun 10am–1pm and 2–6pm, Oct–April 9am–1pm and 2–5pm | admission 2 euros | 🕐 1 hr)* will help you to picture the expansive living quarters and baths. □ N7

OLHÃO

(□ N7) **You will fall in love with the rather idiosyncratic, yet refreshingly tourist-free town of ⭐ Olhão (pop. 14,200) on the Ria Formosa the moment you arrive. The labyrinthine streets of the old town wind their way through tiny, idyllic *praças* and past square white houses, while enormous market halls house countless fish stalls; in the harbour you can see the proof that there are still people here who make their living from fishing.**

It's true, the town also has some ugly parts – the blocks of flats in the outer suburbs are rather depressing, and the fish-processing factories to the east of the port are not particularly pleasant to look at either. But when you take a stroll along the lively waterfront promenade with its many restaurants filling the air with the scent of grilled fish, and take in the "real" Algarvian way of life, then your initial enthusiasm for this place will be confirmed.

SIGHTSEEING

CASA JOÃO LÚCIO

Not a bad gaff! This eccentric "chalet" rises out of the northern edge of the Quinta de Marim. It was built as a weekend retreat by the local poet João Lúcio Pereira (1880–1918), and every staircase, wall and shape within was carefully chosen to fit his eccentric and supernatural view of life. Today, it houses a small museum with changing exhibitions. *Mon–Fri 10am–noon and 2–4pm | admission free | ⏱ 30 mins*

CENTRO DE EDUCAÇÃO AMBIENTAL DE MARIM

At the eastern end of the town, next to a saltworks, you can find the start of an extensive natural reserve in which a wonderful circular trail (4–5km) will introduce you to the beauty of the Ria Formosa lagoon landscape with all its plants and birdlife (keep an eye out for flamingos and storks). The tide mill is awaiting renovation, but at the *visitor centre* you can learn about the natural beauty and habitat of the *ria*. *Park daily*

INSIDER TIP
Wander around the Ria Formosa

Stock up on fresh provisions in the market hall

8.30am–7pm; visitor centre Mon–Fri 9am–5pm | admission 5 euros | Av. Parque Natural Ria Formosa | ⏱ 2 hrs

IGREJA NOSSA SENHORA DO ROSÁRIO

The best feature of this late 16th-century parish church is the fact that you can climb the tower to get an incredible view over the square white houses of the old town with the Ria Formosa in the background. The architecture of these cubic buildings with their flat, terraced roofs is unique in Portugal. Copied by the town's fishermen from buildings they had seen in North Africa, they are slightly reminiscent of the area's Moorish past. The candles in the adjoining *Capela do Senhor dos Aflitos* are lit to ensure the safe return of the fishermen. *Mon–Fri 10–11.30am and 3–5pm | ascent of the tower 1 euro | Praça da Restauração*

MUSEU MUNICIPAL

This small but perfectly formed municipal museum is housed in a building that was formerly home to the local fishermen's fraternity – the late 18th-century *Casa do Compromisso Marítimo*. Alongside displays of archaeological artefacts, it hosts a programme of changing exhibitions on Olhão's cultural history. *Tue–Sat 10am–12.30pm and 1.30–5pm | admission 2.07 euros | Praça da Restauração | ⏱ 30 mins*

EATING & DRINKING

You can find numerous restaurants along the shoreline promenade Avenida 5 de Outubro, all offering superb grilled fish. *O Bote (no. 122 | closed Sun/Mon | tel. 2 89 14 21 02 | €€)* has a particularly traditional feel, while *Pitéu da Baixa Mar (no. 18 | closed Mon and Tue eve | tel. 9 12 06 20 42 | €)* serves good food at a reasonable price. And if you want a change from fish, *Pizza na Pedra (no. 50 | daily | tel. 2 89 70 24 44 | pizza pedra.com | €€)* serves excellent stonebaked pizza. Enjoy!

VAI E VOLTA

José and Maria João's *rodizio* barbecue restaurant has been packing in a huge number of punters for years. Unlike most Brazilian barbecues, the emphasis here is on excellent fish. There is no need to pick things from a menu – waiters bring around different kinds of fish until you can't take any more. It's a great concept if you like fish (and don't mind a bit of a queue – they don't take reservations). *Closed Sun eve and Mon, Sept–May lunch only | Largo do Grémio 2 | vaievolta.pt | €*

SHOPPING

The bustling *market halls (Mon–Sat 7am–1pm | Av. 5 de Outubro)* are one of the highlights of Olhão. You won't find a bigger fish market anywhere on the Algarve and the fruit and veg is great too.

INSIDER TIP
Delicious fish in a beautiful market

There is also a weekly market every Saturday on the square by the market halls, while some nice little shops can be found on the pedestrianised *Rua*

Boardwalks between the dunes of the Ria Formosa, near Olhão

do Comércio. The slightly larger *Ria Shopping Centre (N125 No. 100, riashopping.pt)* pulls in shoppers with its large supermarket, speciality stores and restaurants.

SPORT & ACTIVITIES

What could be better while in Olhão than a visit to the lagoon? A great way to get to know this magical (but fragile) habitat is to take a boat trip with 👥 *Sabino Boattours (tel. 9 15 66 18 60 | sabinoboattours.com).* The crew know the region like the back of their hands and can identify all the local birds as well as explain how to harvest mussels and oysters. They will

even be able to point out the kind of grasses and reeds most enjoyed by seahorses. The five-hour tour includes a delicious lunch break on Culatra.

AROUND OLHÃO

4 CULATRA ⭐

3km from Olhão / 30 mins by ferry to Culatra

If you want to get to Olhão's nearest beaches, then you first need to take a fabulous boat trip. On the quay at the eastern end of the shoreline promenade you will find ferries (for timetables go to *8700-olhao.com*) and pleasure boats that will take you across the lagoon landscape of Ria Formosa to the offshore dune islands of *Armona* and *Culatra (🏛 07–8)*. A few hundred people live here, and most of them work as fishermen or mussel pickers. You won't find any cars here: this is a place to enjoy glorious beaches and plenty of delicious fresh seafood in one of the restaurants. The atmosphere is very friendly all over the islands. The fishing harbour in the main resort, *Culatra*, is especially picturesque. The western edge of the island is called *Ilha do Farol* ("lighthouse island") thanks to the imposing lighthouse built here in 1851. This red and white beauty can be visited on Wednesday afternoons (2–5pm). It might be a long way up but the view from the top over the islands, lagunas and ocean is outstanding. 🏛 N8

5 FUSETA

12km east of Olhão / 20 mins by car on the N125

In this small coastal resort most people head straight for the jetty, from where it's a five-minute trip across the Ria Formosa to *Ilha de Fuseta* with its wonderful sandy beach. The Ilha de Fuseta is actually an extension to the Ilha da Armona, and theoretically you can walk all the way there along the beach (which is surprisingly empty, even in summer). Back on the mainland, you will find a few bars on the waterfront, and delicious grilled fish is available at *Casa Corvo (closed Sun/ Mon | Largo 1° de Maio 1 | tel.* 9 16 12 74 66 | €) near the market hall. Make sure you pay a visit to the church on the outskirts of the village; from its elevated forecourt you can enjoy a beautiful view over Fuseta's white roofs and the *ria*. 🏛 07

6 MONCARAPACHO

13km north of Olhão / 25 mins by car

If you feel the need for something a bit hillier while staying on this extremely flat bit of coast, the *Cerro da Cabeça* is the place to head. Rising up behind the village of Moncarapacho, its porous karst landscape is pockmarked by small craters and deep sinkhole caves. There is a good circular walk (approx. 7km) but not many waymarkers, so keep an eye out. On the way you will see what kind of vegetation survives in this harsh landscape before scrambling up to the highest point for an excellent view over the surrounding region and the Ria Formosa. 🏛 06–7

TAVIRA

(🏛 P6) ⭐ **Tavira is unquestionably the most beautiful town on the Ria Formosa. Its location on the gently flowing Rio Gilão, its many beautiful churches, and the white houses with their hipped roofs that are so typical of Tavira all lend the town a picturesque air.**

In the past, the inhabitants mainly earned their living from salt production and fishing, and in the 15th century the port was an important

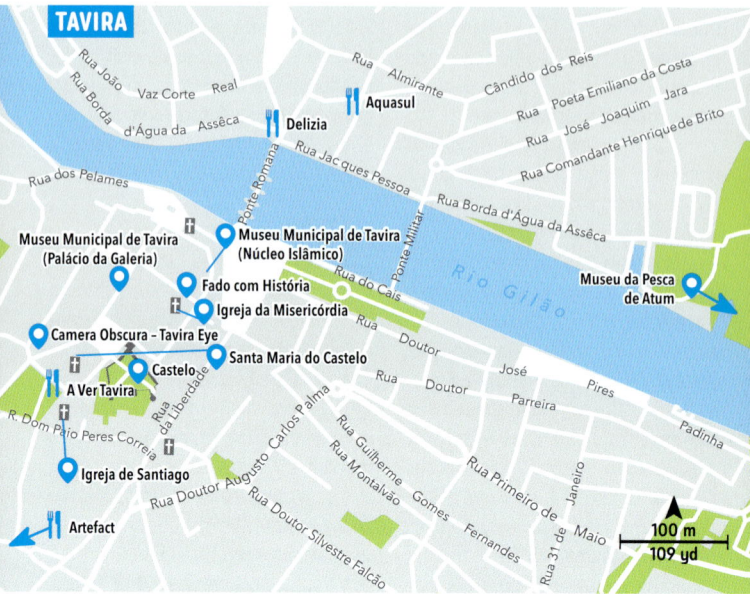

trading post with North Africa. However, Portugal's African colonial possessions were not held for long and in time the port silted up. When the tuna fish also disappeared in the 20th century, Tavira sank into a slumber from which it has only recently been awakened by the tourist industry.

Take your time exploring Tavira (pop. 15,400) on both sides of its river. Potter around the narrow, hilly streets and soak up the town's quiet charm. Wander from one church to the next – there are more than 20 here altogether. Or simply sit back on the beautiful waterfront promenade, under the shade of a palm tree in the idyllic *Jardim Público* next to the old market hall, or in one of the inviting street cafés on the *Praça da República*, and watch the world go by.

And should the need to see the sea grow too strong, jump on a ferry and head out to the *Ilha de Tavira*, with its long sandy beach.

SIGHTSEEING

CAMERA OBSCURA / TAVIRA EYE

A short lesson on optics. Housed in the old water tower, the camera obscura projects live images of Tavira onto a large screen with its lens system. You get a view of the town right across to the salt marshes with a guide telling you all about what you see, including the typical hipped roofs of the old town. *Mon–Fri 11am–3pm | admission 5 euros, children 3 euros | Calçada da Galeria 12 | cameraobscuratavira.com | ⏱ 30 mins*

CASTELO 🐷

Only a few bits of wall from the Moorish fortress have survived, but the *castelo* with its beautifully maintained small garden is still one of the most enchanting places in Tavira. If you have a head for heights, climb up the walls and enjoy the view over the town and the river. *Mon–Fri 8.30am–7pm, Sat/Sun 10am–7pm (winter until 5pm) | admission free | ⏱ 20 mins*

CHURCHES ON THE FORTRESS HILL

Each of the churches mentioned here charges an admission fee of 3 euros; with the 🐷 combi-ticket you pay 7 euros for three churches and 10 euros for five churches. Whatever you do, don't miss the churches around the castle. The harmonious, triple-aisled *Santa Maria do Castelo (Mon–Fri 10am–12.45pm and 2–5.45pm, Sat 10am–12.45pm)* can be spotted from a distance thanks to the enormous clock face on its tower, as well as its elevated position next to the castle. This Gothic church was built on the site of the Moorish mosque during the 13th century, in the wake of the Reconquista, and was given a Manueline extension later on. The 1755 earthquake left its mark but the Gothic entrance portal managed to survive. A second entrance leads to an *exhibition* of sacred art.

From here it's just a short walk to the understated *Igreja de Santiago (Mon–Fri 10am–1pm)* which also dates back to the 13th century. The medallion above the main entrance is interesting in that it depicts São Tiago – St James – on horseback. It is a nod to the fact that the knights of the Order of Santiago, who vanquished the Moors during the conquest of the city in 1242, had occupied the *castelo* after the Reconquista. Inside the church are precious artworks by Portuguese painters that date from the 15th to 18th centuries.

The lavishly decorated *Igreja da Misericórdia (Mon–Fri 10am–1pm, and 2–5.30pm, Sat 10am–12.30pm)* mainly offers 16th-century features: blue and white Rococo *azulejos*, an enormous gilded main altar, and a well-preserved 18th-century cabinet organ balanced on a pedestal that looks as if it is made of marble, but is in fact wooden. You can also visit the vestry and its neighbouring rooms. Make sure you take a look at the Renaissance entrance portal, on which the Mother of God is sheltered by a canopy of stone and flanked by the coats of arms of both Portugal and Tavira.

FADO COM HISTÓRIA

Warning: be prepared for nostalgic music and a sense of yearning. This ambitious cultural association presents 45-minute fado performances either in the *auditório* or the *Igreja da Misericórdia* next door. Visitors are first shown a ten-minute film explaining the history and special features of this melancholic Portuguese genre, before experiencing the passion of its singers and guitarists in a live concert. *Auditório: Mon–Fri 5pm, Mon/Tue and Fri also 3.15pm; Igreja da Misericórdia: Mon–Fri 6.30pm, Sat 5pm, Wed/Thu and Sat 3.15pm | admission 10 euros | Rua Damião Augusto de Brito Vasconcelos 4 | fadocomhistoria.com*

Tavira: the 17th-century Ponte Romana spans the Rio Gilão with its seven arches

MUSEU DA PESCA DE ATUM

Once the biggest tuna-fishing base in the Algarve, today hotel guests occupy the rooms where fishermen used to spend their summers. Decades of overfishing brought an end to the 2,000-year-old industry here in the 1970s, but the small museum explains how these silvery-blue kings and queens of the sea used to be caught and gives advice on delicious ways to cook them. *Daily 9am–9.30pm | free admission | Eco Hotel Vila Galé Albacora, Quatro Águas | ⏱ 20 mins*

MUSEU MUNICIPAL DE TAVIRA

The town museum occupies a number of sites throughout the town, including two chapels and a former water-pumping station. The former residence of the *Palácio da Galeria (Calçada da Galeria)* is worth visiting

for its architecture alone, but it also hosts a changing programme of exhibitions as well as a display of Phoenician artefacts in the atrium. The museum's *Núcleo Islâmico (Praça da Républica)* branch is devoted entirely to archaeology, and is located on the site where remnants of the 12th-century Moorish city wall and a unique vase – the so-called "Vaso de Tavira" – was unearthed in 1996. This unique earthenware pot dates back to the 11th century and its rim is decorated with miniature soldiers, musicians and animals – an incredible find indeed. *Both museums Tue–Sat 9.30am–1pm and 2–4.30pm | admission 2 euros, combined ticket 3 euros | museumunicipaldetavira.cm-tavira.pt | ⏱ 1 hr*

INSIDER TIP
Fabulous find

EATING & DRINKING

AQUASUL

This colourful and playful restaurant situated in the old town on the north bank of the Rio Gilão is decorated with beautiful mosaics – but the art isn't limited to the restaurant's many nooks and crannies (both inside and on the promenade), as the Italian-influenced dishes on the varied menu are also highly creative. Booking essential. *Evening only, closed Sun and Mon | Rua Doutor Augusto Silva Carvalho 11 | tel. 2 81 32 51 66 | €€*

ARTEFACT

You won't see plates of food here, only edible art. It's incredible how creative their tapas are, how artistic the brunch can look and how delicious the *cataplana* tastes. You won't stand a chance without a reservation, since this (French-inspired) gem on the outskirts of town is (sadly) no longer hidden, especially since vegetarians are well catered for too. *Closed Sun and Mon/Tue lunchtimes | Rua das Capacheiras 1 | tel. 9 25 57 21 78 | FB: Artefactavira | €€*

A VER TAVIRA

Of course, when you come here, you're partly paying for the hilltop location and the amazing views over the town from the terrace – but mainly you're paying for chef Luís Brito's Michelin star. Try one of the seasonal tasting menus. *Closed Sun/Mon | Calçada da Galeria 13 | tel. 9 12 95 00 19 | avertavira.com | €€–€€€*

DELIZIA

Probably the best ice cream in the Algarve. On offer are unusual flavours, such as honey, ginger, thyme, carob and fig, but all typical of the Algarve. *Rua 5 de Outubro 9 (Filiale: Mercado da Ribeira) | FB: GelatariasDelizia*

INSIDER TIP
Time for an ice cream

NIGHTLIFE

In summer, there are often festivals and concerts near the former covered market and on the Praça da República, while in winter you're better off heading to the pubs in the old town, such as *Queen's (closed Sun | Rua Almirante Cândido dos Reis 117)* or the Irish pub *The Black Anchor (daily | Rua Borda d'Água da Asseca 46–50 | blackanchortavira.com)*, where you can either watch sport or listen to live bands. If it's liquid happiness you're after, visit *Arcada Cocktail Club (closed Mon | Praça da República 8 | IG: @arcada.cocktail.club)*.

AROUND TAVIRA

🔟 SANTA LUZIA

4km southwest of Tavira / 8 mins by car on the M515

Santa Luzia is best known for octopus fishing, and the harbour promenade with views of the fishing boats is delightful. If you drive another 2km to the *Pedras d'el Rei* holiday resort, you

Spruced up: white and blue tones in Cacela Velha

This beach was also once the site of a tuna-fishing station, and its buildings are now home to a number of cafés and restaurants such as the relaxed *Barril Beach Café (€)* The best thing here is, however, the anchor cemetery. These anchors were formerly used to fix fishing nets in place in the sea. *P7*

INSIDER TIP
Photoshoot in an anchor cemetery

8 ILHA DE TAVIRA

3km from Tavira / 20 mins by ferry

The 10km-long dunes here are uncommonly beautiful. Boats set sail all year round from the *Quatro Águas* station, just outside Tavira, while in summer passengers usually board near Tavira's former indoor market hall. Tavira island has a row of restaurants and a campsite. Unfortunately, the island can be plagued by mosquitoes in the summer, but it is still worth visiting for the incredible beach. *O–P 6–7*

9 CABANAS DE TAVIRA

8km to the east of Tavira / 10 mins by car on the N125

This place may at first sight seem rather unimpressive. However, first impressions can be deceiving. It is in fact the boarding point for a ferry service sailing through the lagoon to the long stretch of beautiful beach at *Praia de Cabanas*. It's a true paradise: on one side you can swim in the warm lagoon water, on the other in the cooler seawater. The resort itself has a welcoming promenade with plenty of (fish) restaurants. *P6*

can then either take a tram or walk along the causeway over the Ria Formosa and through the dunes (1.5km), to get to the wonderful *Praia do Barril* on the Ilha de Tavira.

🔟 CACELA VELHA

12km east of Tavira / 15 mins by car on the N125

A few dozen houses and a small harbour fort dating back to the 12th century, this place has an idyllic setting above the Ria lagoon. Enjoy the views at the esplanade in front of the church, which is also worth a visit. The *village cemetery* is typical of the Algarve region, with coffin drawers stacked one on top of the other. A small and pleasant footpath leads across the sand (and is best used during low tide) to the village of *Fábrica*, 1.5km to the west (also accessible by car). From here, the fishermen will ferry you in their small boats across to the beach on the offshore strips of dunes. (They offer the same service in Cacela Velha.)

📖 Q6

VILA REAL DE SANTO ANTÓNIO

(📖 R5–6) **As you wander through this chic grid-planned town located on the Rio Guadiana by the Spanish border, you will immediately notice that the atmosphere here is different to other holiday resorts. Vila Real is a typical border town, and Spanish people come here to do their shopping, while day-trippers visit to see the town that was personally designed in the 18th century by the Marquês de Pombal, Prime Minister of Portugal.**

The king at the time was unhappy that the border region was so sparsely populated, and he also wanted to supervise the trade of goods across the Rio Guadiana and the fishing industry in Monte Gordo after the 1755 earthquake. As a result, over the course of five months in 1774, he erected this "Royal City" on the site of the small fishing village of Santo António de Avelinha. His supervision plan didn't quite work out as intended: the relatively well-off fishermen in nearby Monte Gordo refused to move and decided instead to join with Spain, purely to escape the clutch of the customs authorities.

Nowadays, VRSA (as the Portuguese like to refer to the border town) is home to around 11,750 people. The bustling town centre with its grid layout is ideal for exploring on foot. Start on the Avenida da República, the grand avenue running along the sea-front with its yacht harbour and weighty statue of the town's founder, the Marquês de Pombal. The *main square* with its star-shaped paving and adjoining church and town hall is named after him and forms the centre point of the town. From here, you will find your way with ease into all the busy shopping streets. The inviting stores and large selection of textiles and household items are very popular with Spaniards who stream in by ferry or via the motorway bridge.

EATING & DRINKING

A row of restaurants can be found in the extensive pedestrian precinct on the *Avenida da República*. They are all good and reasonably priced. The town's Spanish neighbours are aware of this and the spectacular waterfront is where they come to hang out.

ASSOCIAÇÃO NAVAL

Welcome to the yacht club – stylish atmosphere directly on the Rio Guadiana, serving fresh, top-quality seafood and with a large selection of tapas. *Daily | Av. da República | tel. 2 81 51 30 38 | associacaonavaldo guadiana.pt | €€*

BEACHES

The *Praia da Ponta da Areia* and *Praia de Santo António* just by the pier at the mouth of the river are still relatively untouched by human development. If you want beaches with the kind of infrastructure that comes with development, head to the resort of *Monte Gordo* (pop. 3,200), 4km to the west. With a host of concrete hotels, it is not going to win any prizes for beauty but if they were to give out prizes for lovely beaches with great views of fishing boats out at sea, it would be in with a good chance.

The ✴ *Praia Verde* more than lives up to its name. Seven kilometres west of VRSA, this "green beach" is tucked away among dunes covered in vegetation. The former fishing village of *Manta Rota,* 4km further to the west, is more relaxed than Monte Gordo. In general, the beaches around VRSA are quieter than the those on the rocky part of the Algarve coast. And if you have had enough of Portuguese beaches by this point … there are plenty to explore just across the border in Spain.

SPORT & ACTIVITIES

The wooded dunes are a dream for those wanting to exercise even in the heat of the  summer. You can walk or even jog with a good sea breeze and a bit of shade to stop you from overheating.

INSIDER TIP
A walk in the woods

Along the coast between Vila Real de Santo António and Monte Gordo is a small natural park, the *Mata Nacional das Dunas Litorais*, which is particularly important for the conservation of chameleons.

If you feel like swinging from branch to branch, the 😺 *Parque Aventura (parqueaventura.net/vrsa)* offers a great fun space to explore the treetops. An ideal place to keep anyone with lots of energy entertained.

The moment you see the Rio Guadiana, you will find its allure hard to escape and a 😺 boat trip is a must. Climb aboard to explore this highly fertile valley filled with groves of olives, oranges, figs and lemons on all sides. Between them, their lifeblood – the silvery tidal river – flows to *Mértola*. Sailors like to anchor in this river as there are no overnight fees. There are several companies offering boat tours (often including lunch). Two good options are *TransGuadiana*

A boat tour on the Rio Guadiana provides views of the Ponte Internacional do Guadiana

(transguadiana.com) and *Rio Sul (rio-sultravel.com)*. Most companies will take you to *Alcoutim* or out to *Foz de Odeleite* and back.

WELLNESS

Unlike much of the Mediterranean, there are few hot springs in the Algarve. As a result, it feels even more luxurious when you take a salt bath at *Spa Salino* in the *Água Mãe (summer daily 10am–6pm, August 9am–7pm | Salina Barquinha, Castro Marim | FB: aguamae)*. *Água Mãe* does not only produce table salt, it also uses it for a huge variety of spa activities and treatments, from yoga on a salt flat to salt-based facemasks.

NIGHTLIFE

In summer, nearby *Monte Gordo* is the hub of the area's nightlife. The *casino* has a relaxed atmosphere. Bars and clubs are open until the early hours.

AROUND VILA REAL DE SANTO ANTÓNIO

11 CASTRO MARIM
4km north of Vila Real de Santo António / 5 mins by car on the N122
This town of 3,300 inhabitants is

There are superb views from the *castelo* at Castro Marim

entirely dedicated to its castle(s). In the 14th century, this "coastal fort" was the headquarters for the powerful Order of Christ, which was headed by Prince Henry the Navigator from the beginning of the 15th century. The well-preserved ruins of the *castelo (daily 9.30am–1pm and 3–6.30pm, Nov–March 9am–1pm and 2–5pm | admission 1.10 euros)*, are a reminder of a period of great splendour. The fortress protected the border with Spain well into the 17th century. These ruins serve as the backdrop to *Dias Medievais* or "medieval days", a fantastic historical festival that takes place at the end of August. The castle parapet gives you a full view of its counterpart *Forte de São Sebastião* on a hill nearby (closed to visitors) as well

as the Rio Guadiana's expansive estuary and saltworks. 📖 *R5*

🄬 RESERVA NATURAL DO SAPAL DE CASTRO MARIM

Information centre 8km north of Vila Real de Santo António / 13 mins by car

One of Portugal's most important wetland areas lies in the estuary of the Rio Guadiana. Two-thirds of the approximately 21km² area is covered in water and it is a favoured breeding ground for many aquatic bird species, among them flamingos. Many migratory birds also come here in the winter. Birdwatching is possible near the *information centre* (close to the motorway bridge) and around the salt marshes. 📖 *R5–6*

🔟 ALCOUTIM ⭐

40km north of Vila Real de Santo António / 35 mins by car on the IC 27/N122-1

The drive to Alcoutim via the Odeleite reservoir is by far and away the prettiest way to get there. Alcoutim is technically a small town but, with a population of around 1,100, it has a distinctly sleepy villagey feel. The 14th-century *castelo (daily 9am–5pm, summer 10am–7pm | admission 3 euros | ⏱ 30 mins)* is charming rather than imposing. Dating back to the 16th century, the *Igreja Matriz* is also an interesting sight, being one of the Algarve's first Renaissance churches.

Situated 8km further south, the *Museo do Rio (Tue–Sat 9am–1pm, 2–5pm (summer 10am–1pm, 2–6pm | admission 3 euros (🐖 included in the ticket to the castelo) | Guerreiros do Rio | ⏱ 30 mins)* provides an insight into the people living on the Rio Guadiana and the central role of fishing and smuggling in this area. The ferry takes you to Spain in no time, and from here you have a better view of the white town. Those after an adrenaline kick can even ✅ zipline over the border from Spain (see also p. 136).

Freshwater swimming in a dammed river is possible at the attractive beach of *Praia Fluvial Pego Fundo* (signposted). Enjoy a meal afterwards on the village square in the restaurant *O Camané (closed Tue | tel. 9 64 10 85 85 | €–€€)* or enjoy tapas at *Beira Rio (closed Wed | Av. Duarte Pacheco 8 | tel. 9 63 13 90 28 | €)*.

Alcoutim is the starting point of the *Via Algarviana*, a long-distance hiking trail which takes walkers for more than 300km through the hinterland to *Cabo de São Vicente*. There are also plenty of other pretty footpaths and circular walks nearby. 📖 R2

THE
BARLAVENTO

PICTURE-PERFECT ROCKY BAYS

The otherworldly cliffs on this rocky coastline glow in every shade of red and yellow and provide the perfect natural frame for a classic Algarve photo. The cliffs surround the idyllic sandy coves of the Western Algarve, known as the Barlavento, or "windward" coast, considered to be one of the most beautiful beach landscapes in Europe.

Over the millennia, the wind and the waves have sculpted the soft limestone cliffs into incredible shapes and stunning little coves,

Ponta da Piedade: the Algarve is famous for its striking rocky coastline

where visitors often have to descend narrow wooden steps in order to reach the clear, turquoise water. The landscape also opens up at certain points, with longer sandy beaches appearing at the mouths of rivers. Around these, some of the region's thriving tourist hubs have developed, with golf courses, shops and nightclubs to keep you occupied at all hours of the day. A paradise for those into beach life and nightlife, the Barlavento is also a great destination if you're looking for water sports or spectacular coastal walks.

THE BARLAVENTO

MARCO POLO HIGHLIGHTS

★ **LAGOS**
Harbour town with a golden chapel, a rich history and plenty of bars ➤ p. 70

★ **PONTA DA PIEDADE**
A lighthouse, ochre-coloured cliffs and amazing rock formations ➤ p. 72

★ **ALVOR**
Old fishing town with a huge beach, a lagoon and an ornate church portal ➤ p. 84

★ **FERRAGUDO**
Picturesque fishing village at the mouth of the Rio Arade ➤ p. 84

MARCO POLO BUCKET LIST

3 ✔ Paddle through grottoes

Glide in a sea kayak through the beaches and caves of the *Ponta da Piedade* ➤ p. 76

4 ✔ Breathe underwater and be amazed

Learn to dive with *Blue Ocean Divers* in Lagos and discover fish and a shipwreck or two ➤ p. 76

Santa Clara-a-Velha

Pardieiros

Monchique

Alferce

Marmelete

90km, 1 hr

The shopping centre and beach boutiques in Portimão are the perfect place to go shopping, as it's the only biggish city in the area besides Faro.

Albufeira de Odeáxere

1 Barragem da Bravura

120

A22

Bensafrim

Mexilhoeira Grande

266

2 Zoo de Lagos

Odiáxere

Barão de São João

Portimão
p. 78

Monte Judeu

6 Alvor

Praia de Alvor

Barão de São Miguel

7

Ferragudo ★

Budens

Lagos ★
p. 70

4 ✔

3 Luz

Praia Dona Ana

4 Burgau

Ponta da Piedade ★

✔ **3**

5 Salema

Lagos offers the perfect mix of hotels, restaurants and bars, beautiful beaches and great sporting options (including water sports) – it's an ideal place to stay if you want to discover the western Algarve.

Beach hopping deluxe: between Luz and Vilamoura, every few metres you will find yet another spectacular rocky cove with the finest sand; you can choose a different one every day.

O C E A N O

★ **ALBUFEIRA**
Party atmosphere, lively night scene, great beaches ➤ p. 87

★ **VILAMOURA**
Chic yachting hotspot for the rich and famous ➤ p. 95

★ **NOSSA SENHORA DA ROCHA**
Could it be more photogenic? A white chapel perched high on the red-orange cliffs ➤ p. 92

The area around Albufeira is the most central location in the Algarve. From here, you can easily get to all corners of the region via the motorway and national roads.

90km, 1 hr

48km, 1 hr

9.5km, 3½ hrs

Carvoeiro

Praia da Marinha

Nossa Senhora da Rocha ★

Lagoa dos Salgados

Armação de Pêra

Many of the beaches in the rocky Algarve can only be reached via steps (and some only from the sea by kayak). If you've got a lot to carry or you're not so sure-footed, check in advance how steep it's going to be!

Albufeira ★
p. 87

Want to party hard and don't mind being surrounded by English tourists? Then the centre of Albufeira is the place to be.

Praia da Falésia

Vilamoura ★

A T L Â N T I C O

4 km
2.49 mi

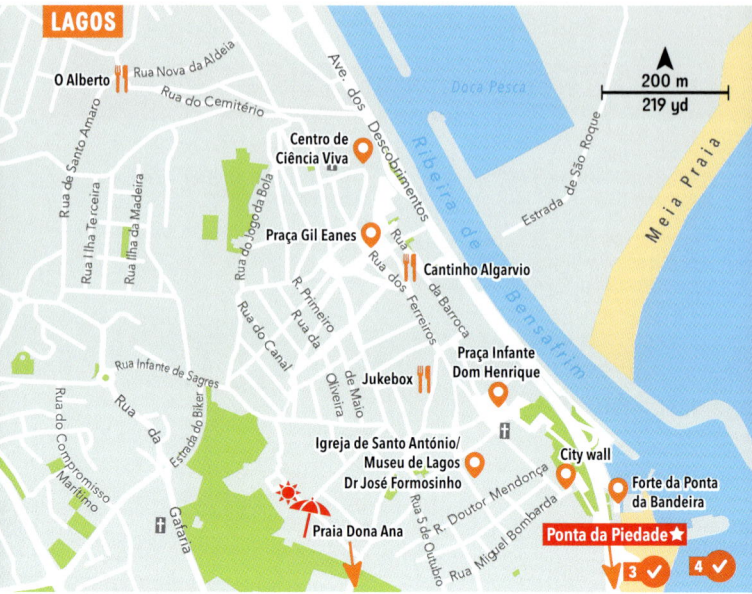

LAGOS

(□ E6–7) **Welcome to ⭐ Lagos! Whether you take a stroll through the lively streets of the old town, go for a swim on the long sandy beach or in the various small coves nearby, or take to the water to explore the unique grottoes and rocky pinnacles of the Ponta da Piedade, you'll feel as if you're in paradise! What's more, the former capital of the Algarve also has plenty of history and culture to offer.**

The mouth of the Ribeira de Bensafrim served as a sheltered mooring for the Phoenicians before the city of Lacobriga was founded here in the Roman period. Today, Lagos (pop. 23,650) is the most important town on the coast of the western Algarve; as you wander through the old town, which is still almost entirely encircled by a city wall, you will find many traces of its former significance, including statues that hark back to Portugal's Age of Discovery. At that time, Lagos was the last safe harbour that ships could call at before heading into the stormy Atlantic. Henry the Navigator sent forth his caravels from here onto the world's oceans in the 15th century, and at various points thereafter the majority of Portugal's trade with the rest of the world was conducted via Lagos. However, this is also where the decline of Portugal's Golden Age began. In 1578, the young King Sebastião had the misguided idea to fight Islam in Morocco. He set off from Lagos with 20,000 soldiers. Only a few returned, and the king was not among them. Portugal subsequently became a Spanish province for 60 years and, by the time it became independent once again, the English and Dutch had picked its colonial empire to pieces. With the earthquake in 1755, this once great city's downfall was complete – it only began to regain its identity with the advent of tourism in the 20th century.

SIGHTSEEING

CITY WALL

You can gain a hugely varied perspective on Lagos by taking a walk along the astonishingly well-preserved city wall. Its current form dates back to the 16th century, but a defensive boundary was already in place during Roman and Moorish times. The most representative section can be found in the small *Jardim da Constituição* park between the Praça Infante Dom Henrique and the *Arco de São Gonçalo*, an attractive Moorish gate, which today bears the name of the town's patron saint. If you walk along the western section of the *muralha* you will scarcely find any tourists; here, the narrow streets of the old town grow increasingly quiet and very few of the buildings have been spruced up. Local residents walk their dogs in the patches of green behind the walls. It is worth getting to know this "other" side of Lagos – if only to see the works of local street artists on many of the walls in this part of town.

CENTRO DE CIÊNCIA VIVA

Engage their hands, their brains and their imagination! This interactive science museum, housed in a colourful pink building from the 17th century, teaches kids what the Portuguese journeys of discovery were all about. They can also find out how to communicate at sea and discover how a submarine works – plus much more besides! It's playful and fun for family members at all ends of the age spectrum. *Tue–Sun 10am–6pm | admission 5 euros, children (6–17) 3 euros | Rua Dr Faria e Silva 34 (above the covered market) | lagos.cienciaviva.pt | ⏱ 1 hr*

The imposing Forte da Ponta da Bandeira was built to protect Lagos's harbour

FORTE DA PONTA DA BANDEIRA

The 17th-century builders of this fort certainly knew what they were doing. Tucked in at the point where the harbour's canal flows into the city, it could not have been better placed to protect the city from pirates. Ideal for defence back then, its location also means that it has superb views of the rocky cliffs and soft sand combination that makes Lagos such an attractive place today. A drawbridge leads into the well-preserved fortress, which contains a small, *azulejo*-lined chapel. *Tue–Sun 10am–1pm and 2–6pm* | 🐷 *admission free* | 🕐 *20 mins*

IGREJA DE SANTO ANTÓNIO/ MUSEU DE LAGOS DR JOSÉ FORMOSINHO

The municipal museum of Lagos is referred to by some people as the "attic museum", as it apparently displays everything that has ever been unearthed in the attics of the town. It's true, the exhibits are something of a mish-mash, but that doesn't do justice to the varied displays you can find here, and recent renovations mean it is now a wonderful place to explore. There are artefacts from the Roman and Muslim eras, as well as coins, sacred art, paintings, traditional clothing, models of farms and fisheries, and much more besides. However, the undoubted highlight is the 18th-century Baroque *chapel of St Anthony*, which is only accessible via the museum. With its opulent *talha dourada* (gilded wood carving) and *azulejos*, its interior is one of the most magnificent on the Algarve. The paintings along the walls depict the miracles of St Anthony of Padua, who was born in Lisbon in 1195 and is extremely popular in Portugal. *Tue–Sun 10am–1pm and 2–6pm | admission 3 euros; combined ticket with Rota da Escravatura 5 euros | Rua General Alberto Carlos da Silveira |* 🕐 *1 hr*

PONTA DA PIEDADE ⭐

The colourful magnificence of the Algarve coast in all its geological diversity … and all in one place. Exploring the wonderful landscape of "Piety Point" on foot should be on every Algarve itinerary, especially for keen photographers. Narrow paths and new wooden walkways run along the edge of the red cliffs, which reach up to 40m high in places, while steep staircases take you down to stunning coves such as *Praia Dona Ana* and *Praia do Camilo*. But the highlight of this narrow promontory is the lighthouse on its tip, which sits majestically above craggy cliffs that are characterised by grottoes, caves and towering rocks. If you follow the stairs down from the lighthouse, you will find a truly extraordinary jetty tucked into a cave. If the tide is right, there is nowhere better to start a boat trip along the coast (see p. 76).

PRAÇA GIL EANES

This square causes confusion, and not because of the sheer number of cafés and shops in the alleyways round about that can be disorienting. The real problem arises from the square's name and the statue at its centre. The

Henry the Navigator lords it over the central Praça Infante Dom Henrique in Lagos

praça is named after the Lagos native Gil Eanes, who – under Henry the Navigator's influence – was the first person to sail round Cape Bojador, in 1434. But the statue in the square depicts the far more tragic figure of King Sebastian. Erected in 1970 by the frequently misunderstood sculptor João Cutileiro, the statue seems almost child-like and makes the king look more like Saint-Exupéry's *Little Prince* or even a young astronaut than an all-powerful ruler. The town's only memorial to Gil Eanes is a bronze statue in the *Jardim da Constituição*.

PRAÇA INFANTE DOM HENRIQUE

Henrique, or Henry the Navigator sits proudly in the middle of Lagos's central square, surveying his surroundings and checking out the view all the way down to the Meia Praia. The sea view may seem apt, but it is likely it would have turned the famous navigator king green – he suffered badly from seasickness. Several historic buildings line the *praça*: in the direction of the sea lies the former *governor's palace* (seat of Algarve governors from the 14th century onwards). The small Manueline window at the far right is reputed to be where Sebastian made his final address to the people before setting out on his fatal expedition to North Africa – his failure to return meant the Portuguese throne was left empty, ready for the Spanish to take over. On the right of the palace is the Baroque *Igreja Santa Maria*.

To the left of the large white customs house at the northern end of the square stands the former *slave market*. This is where the first official sale of people from sub-Saharan Africa took place in 1444, marking the beginning of the European slave trade at the start of the colonial period. This dark chapter in the city's history is traced in the *Rota de Escavratura*, a small, interactive museum *(Tue–Sun 10am–1pm and 2–6pm | admission 3 euros, combined ticket with Museu de Lagos 5 euros | ⏱ 30 mins)*. During construction of the underground car park to the north of the square, excavations revealed the human remains of a large number of people of African descent and evidence of the brutality of the slave trade. It seems likely that slaves who had died on the journey from Africa were simply thrown overboard on arrival. The same excavations also uncovered 3,000-year-old sandstone blocks that the Phoenicians had used to construct the town's first quay.

INSIDER TIP
Hidden ancient harbour wall

Crystal-clear water, super-fine sand and golden cliffs at Praia Dona Ana

EATING & DRINKING

CANTINHO ALGARVIO

It's often difficult to find a table in this charming and long-established restaurant in the pedestrian zone – and it's easy to understand why once you've tasted the delicious seafood on offer here. *Closed Sat lunchtime and Sun | Rua Afonso d'Almeida 17 | tel. 2 82 76 12 89 | FB: O Cantinho Algarvio | €€*

JUKEBOX

Fancy some *petiscos* (tapas)? Book a table in minutes via WhatsApp and head off to Jukebox, where you can try bite-sized portions of Portuguese cuisine. There's plenty for vegetarians too. *Closed lunchtime and Mon | Rua Soeiro da Costa 40a | tel. 9 10 57 10 11 | FB: jukeboxbudget | €*

O ALBERTO

Guests here can see for themselves that everything is cooked from scratch. Watching Alberto at work in the kitchen is generally more entertaining than watching the TV shows that play in the background at this typical Portuguese restaurant. Delicious *cataplanas*, as well as fish and meat dishes, are brought to the table by Dona Odette herself. *Closed Sun/Mon and lunchtime | Largo Convento Senhora Glória 27 | tel. 2 82 76 93 87 | restauranteoalberto.pt | €€*

SHOPPING

The old town is chock-a-block full of small shops. A lot of them (perhaps even the majority) sell mostly tourist tat, but there are great things to be found too. For particularly beautiful ceramics, head to *Galeria JJ Mealha (Rua Dr José Cabrita 3 | FB: MealhaCeramics).* The *indoor market hall (Av. dos Descobrimentos)* is well worth a visit, especially if you are after some fresh produce: fish is sold on the ground floor, and fruit and vegetables are on the first floor. From the roof terrace, there's a view of the marina.

BEACHES

Stretching out to the east of Lagos is *Meia Praia* – a vast sandy beach that goes on for kilometres beyond the railway line (fortunately not a big distraction), curving all the way to the Ria de Alvor. Surfers, kitesurfers and windsurfers alike love the swell that you get here. Directly alongside the harbour fort is where the beaches of the Ponta da Piedade begin, from ✈ *Praia Dona Ana* (a favourite because of its unusual rocks) to *Praia do Camilo*.

To the west of the Ponta lies *Porto Mós*, a slightly larger bay surrounded by cliffs with a beautiful beach. The *Praia da Luz* is similarly wide and very popular in summer. The further west you go, the emptier and more secluded the beaches become.

SPORT & ACTIVITIES

Everywhere in Lagos you can buy tickets for ☺ boat trips to the grottoes of the Ponta da Piedade. Whether you choose to relax aboard a sailing boat with *Bom Dia Boat Trips (bomdiaboat trips.com)*, or opt for the sporty option and hire a ✔ kayak (from e.g. *kayaklagos.pt*) or a stand-up paddleboard (from e.g. *nowhere2far.com*) – exploring this rocky coast is a must! There's a lot to see under the water too, for example with Elmar and Ute's ✔ *diving school (blue-ocean-divers.eu)*. Enjoy mini golf? By the western gate of the city walls a minigolf course sits resplendent on the roof of a multi-storey car park. It is remarkably tasteful, with small ponds and modern art in between the holes *(proputtinggarden. com)*.

INSIDER TIP
Rooftop minigolf

NIGHTLIFE

Things kick off in the evenings along the alleyways north of Praça Infante Dom Henrique (as well as on the roof of the car park). This is where you will find the highest density of bars and music cafés, with live music pumping from many venues at weekends (especially in the summer). For a nice cocktail, make a detour to see Rick and Rozy at *The Star (Wed–Mon 7pm–2am | Travessa 1 de Maio 9 | FB: TheStar. Lagos)*; here, Monday is quiz night, Saturday is rock night and Sunday is karaoke night.

AROUND LAGOS

◼ BARRAGEM DA BRAVURA

15km north of Lagos / 20 mins by car on the N125/N125-9

A charming trail – especially in the spring when the meadows are in bloom – leads you via *Odiáxere* to this reservoir, constructed in 1958. It is surrounded by forested hills that are ideal for a picnic or for hiking. 🗺 *D–E5*

◼ ZOO DE LAGOS ☺

12km northwest of Lagos / 17 mins by car on the N125/M532-1

Exotic animals, including birds and primates, are kept in species-appropriate surroundings in this charming and well-maintained private zoo. The kangaroos, for example, leap around a large enclosure with plenty of space, while peacocks strut along the paths and flamingos balance on one leg in the zoo's own small lake. The petting zoo allows smaller visitors an opportunity to meet the animals up close and personally. *Sítio do Medronhal | Barão de São João | April–Sept daily 10am–7pm, Oct–March daily 10am–5pm | admission 19 euros, children (3-11) 14 euros | zoolagos. com | ▥ D6*

3 LUZ

8km west of Lagos / 12 mins by car on the N125

Sadly, the resort of Luz (pop. 4,450) is forever associated in many people's minds with the disappearance of Maddie McCann, the young girl that went missing here during a family holiday in 2007. If you can set the tragedy aside, then the town has plenty to offer visitors – a stunning beach, a small chapel, numerous welcoming restaurants and a

charming promenade lined with lampposts and palm trees where exca-vations have revealed the remains of a Roman site. ▥ *D7*

4 BURGAU

13km west of Lagos / 20 mins by car on the N125

In this old, surprisingly authentic fish-ing village (especially compared to the much more touristy Luz), you'll find a small beach and pleasant bars where you can stop for a bite to eat. The surrounding countryside is largely unspoilt , and you can hike along the cliffs to the ruins of the 17th-century *Forte de Almádena* close to the *Praia da Boca do Rio* (approx. 3km). Archaeological finds have proved that this small estuary was settled by the Romans. ▥ *D7*

There's a relaxed holiday atmosphere on the beach promenade at Luz

5 SALEMA

20km west of Lagos / 25 mins by car on the N125

This coastal village is nestled in a little valley so idyllic that, back in the day, even dinosaurs came to visit – their footprints can still be seen in the rocks on the beach. The beach is flanked on either side by huge, dramatic cliffs. A good spot from which to watch the sun go down while tucking into delicious Portuguese food is *A Boia (closed Mon | Rua dos Pescadores 101 | tel. 2 82 69 53 82 | FB: boiabar | €€).* *C7*

Why were sardines canned?
The Museu de Portimão has the answer

PORTIMÃO

(F6) **The Algarve's second "proper" city after Faro is fascinating and full of contrasts. Down by the sea, the glorious Praia da Rocha gleams in the sun; the Rio Arade is busy with boats and there's a great museum; while the historic centre, which is largely untouched by tourists, offers a perfectly normal (and perhaps slightly run-down) inner-city atmosphere.**

With its many featureless modern buildings and roads, *Portimão* (pop. 49,200) may at first seem rather ugly and unappealing. However, look more closely and you'll find some great areas, such as the beach of *Praia da Rocha* or, for example, pretty *Jardim Visconde Bivar*, a park in the attractive palm-lined *Zona Ribeirinha* along the river.

The Phoenicians knew the Arade estuary as a good place to moor their ships, and the Romans named the settlement Portus Magnus, or great harbour. Today, the marina is one of the biggest in Portugal, and anyone travelling to the Algarve by cruise ship will dock in Portimão. Small shipyards and the fishing industry still play a role, and even though there is only one cannery left, the lively Sardine Festival that is celebrated in August is a sign of what is important to the people who live here.

PORTIMÃO

Pedra Mourinha

Avenida São João de Deus

Taberna da Maré

Dona Barca

Ponte Velha

A Casa da Isabel

Teatro Municipal de Portimão

Rua Direita

O Mané

Estrada de Alvor

Avenida V7

Avenida Miguel Bombarda

Rua Dom Carlos I

Avenida Guanaré

Ribeirinha

Rua da Cruz Vermelha

Avenida São Lourenço da Barrosa (V6)

Avenida do Brasil

Museu de Portimão

Avenida 25 de Abril

Rua Sidónio Pais

Arade

Rua Jaime Palhinha

Avenida Engenheiro Francisco Bívar

Estrada da Rocha

Praia de Alvor

Variante 8

Rua da Falésia

Avenida das Comunidades Lusíadas

Super Juice

Praia da Rocha

Avenida Tomás Cabreira

Avenida Rio Arade

Nana's Bar

400 m
437 yd

SIGHTSEEING

MUSEU DE PORTIMÃO

Where industry and culture meet! This former fish-canning factory has been converted into a municipal museum that has managed to retain the building's architectural interest while also creating a fantastic local museum. It is well worth a visit – and not just when it's raining. The old machinery and an impressive film from 1946 show you how the cannery used to operate, and how the female workforce packed the sardines into tins. You will also learn all kinds of fascinating facts about fishing and agriculture in this region, as well as about its prehistoric inhabitants. There is also a changing programme of exhibitions on the top floor and in the old cistern in the cellar. *Tue 2.30–6pm, Wed–Sun 10am–6pm, mid-July–end Aug Tue–Sun 3–11pm | admission 3 euros | Rua Dom Carlos | museudeportimao.pt | ⏱ 1½ hrs*

PEDRA MOURINHA

If you feel the need to see something seriously strange, make a trip out to the industrial zone, *Pedra Mourinha*:

on Rua de Pedra 5 there is a large boulder, about 4m long, jutting out of the pavement. Geologists believe  that the rock originally came from the Serra de Monchique, so how on earth did it end up here? Nobody knows! In the absence of a scientific answer, generations of theories have led to a popular local legend: a Moorish princess fell in love with a peasant boy in this area. When her father, the king, heard about the relationship, he immediately packed the boy off to war where he died near Monchique. The princess went to the site and her tears flowed all the way down from the mountains to Portimão where they solidified into a rock … not a happy ending.

INSIDER TIP
Stray rock

PRAIA DA ROCHA ⚑

When people talk about the "beach of the rock", they don't just mean the marvellous long and wide sandy beach that separates Portimão from the Atlantic; rather, they are referring to an entire district of the city that was developed at the beginning of the 20th century as a fashionable spa resort, complete with Art Deco villas and the first casino on the Algarve. Unfortunately, it has been rather defaced over the decades with a good deal of concrete; nonetheless, you can still wander along the beach for several kilometres and take advantage of countless cafés and bars. During the summer the whole place is packed. At the eastern end, near the mouth of the Rio Arade, the 17th-century harbour fortress, the *Fortaleza de Santa Catarina*, offers splendid views over the modern marina and across the river to Ferragudo. At the western end of the beach, the *Miradouro dos Três Castelos* sits on a promontory and provides glorious views of the *praias*.

A CASA DA ISABEL

A visit to this tiny, traditional café is always worthwhile – if only for the decorative *azulejo* façade. But then you'll spot the vast quantities of home-made delicacies … it's a dream! Don't leave without sampling Isabel's Trilogia Algarvia – a wonderfully sweet treat made from carob, almonds and figs. *Closed Wed | Rua Direita 61 | tel. 2 82 48 43 15 | acasa daisabel.com | €*

INSIDER TIP
A trio of tastes in a single dessert

Fresh produce from the surrounding fields is available at the market hall in Portimão

DONA BARCA

They turn up the heat in this restaurant located under the old Arade bridge in order to serve up freshly grilled fish daily. In our opinion, this is the best place to get smoky grilled sardines in the summer. *Closed Tue | Largo da Barca | tel. 2 82 48 41 89 | €€*

O MANÉ

This untouristy place serving meat and seafood dishes is extremely popular with the locals. Give the delicious *Massada de Peixe* a try, it'sa stew made up of fish and pasta, or go for the excellent *Carne de Porco à Alentejano*, a pork dish served with mussels. *Closed Sun evenings and Mon | Largo Doutor Bastos 1 | tel. 2 82 42 34 96 | | FB: Restaurante O Mane | €–€€*

SUPER JUICE

Sure, Luís and Anna's team can mix you incredibly delicious, fresh smoothies and juices. But they can also make you substantial protein shakes, fruity açaí bowls and healthy snacks (including vegan options). And if you're really hungry, you can order a hearty "Buddha bowl" to fill you right up. *Daily 9am–6pm, Fri/Sat and summertime until 8pm | Av. Tomás Cabreira, Edif. Casa da Praia, Loja 16 | tel. 9 26 85 44 18 | IG: @rochasuperjuice | €*

INSIDER TIP
Juice it up!

TABERNA DA MARÉ

While you wait for your food at this traditional tavern, you can admire a collection of old photos that show you what Portimão looked like in days gone by. One of the best things on the menu is the grilled squid. *Closed Mon and Tue | Travessa da Barca 9 | tel. 2 82 41 46 14 | FB: tabernadamare | €–€€*

SHOPPING

Countless shops can be found in the alleyways between the Praça da República, Igreja Matriz and the river-bank, and while you explore, you'll also be getting to know Portimão's historical centre. The city's *covered market (Mon–Fri 7am–2pm and 5–8pm, Sat 7am–2pm | Av. São João de Deus)* is the most modern in the Algarve with plenty of fresh local produce.

At the *Parque de Feiras e Exposições* beyond the railway tracks there's a regional market on the first Monday of the month and a flea market on the first and third Sunday of the month. You can find colourful contemporary art in the impressive gallery *Lady in Red (Mon–Sat 10am–6pm | Rua Infante Dom Henrique 140 | galerialadyinred.com)*.

The *Aqua Portimão* is a massive shopping centre with more than 130 shops, cinemas, restaurants, a large supermarket and lots of activities. It is on the main road into Portimão, so it is hard to miss.

BEACHES

No doubt about it: the ⚑ *Praia da Rocha* beach is the best advert for Portimão, thanks to its fine, soft sand and the long, wooden promenade that passes many beach bars. There's lots going on here in summer, including beach volleyball and all sorts of water sports.

Climb aboard the *Santa Bernarda* for a tour of the coast

To the west are smaller bays with magnificent beaches protected by rocks: *Praia dos Três Castelos*, *Praia do Vau* or *Praia do Alemão*. There are also tiny sections of coast here that are difficult to access, such as *Praia do Caniço* near the Prainha resort with it's *Restaurant-Bar Caniço (April–Oct | tel. 2 82 45 85 03 | canicorestaurante. com | €€)*, nestled between the rocks on the beach. The coastal landscape opens up again just at the point where the 🐾 *Praia de Alvor* begins. This huge beach is backed by dunes, which separate it from a lagoon that is home to a large number of interesting birds. Walk along the dunes for beautiful views of the Ria de Alvor.

SPORT & ACTIVITIES

All aboard! You can take some wonderful boat trips from Portimão, exploring the caves along the cliffs or up the river to Silves; the pleasure-boat moorings are located on the waterfront by the beautiful *Jardim Visconde Bivar* park. For an extra-special experience, try taking a trip on the two-masted cutter 🐵 *Santa Bernarda (tickets 38 euros, children aged 3 to 10 years 20 euros | see website for departure times | tel. 9 67 02 38 40 | santa-bernarda.com)*, which has been converted into a caravel worthy of any pirate and is moored on the *Cais Vasco da Gama*. Its passengers can also embark on an exciting cave expedition in inflatable dinghies. For romantics, the late afternoon sunset tour is recommended (only in midsummer).

If you would like to see the underwater world, then a snorkelling trip is just the thing. Inês and Pedro from *Zip & Trip (half day 63 euros | tel. 9 29 25 93 48 | zipandtripalgarve.com)* offer bespoke and varied trips to sea caves.

If you are more into soaring in the sky than diving to the depths, the airport in Montes de Alvor may well offer you a perfect day out. The airfield is mainly used by a sky-diving company, *Skydive Algarve (from 139 euros | tel. 9 14 26 68 32 | skydivealgarve.com)*, who will help you tick one unforgettable experience off your bucket list. **INSIDER TIP It's raining people** In tandem with an experienced skydiver, you will leap from a plane at a dizzying height.

Children (and more than a few adults) will be in heaven at the the waterpark 🐵 *Slide & Splash (April–Oct, opening hours vary so check online | admission 27 euros, children aged 1 month to 10 years from 20 euros, 🐦 online discount | Lagoa | slidesplash.com | 🕐 plan a whole day!)*. The huge slides are designed for you to go fast so **INSIDER TIP Slide safely** we strongly advise women to wear a well-fitting bikini or a full swimming costume.

NIGHTLIFE

Parallel to the beach, you will find plenty of pubs, sports bars and cocktail places in *Praia da Rocha* – some only open in summer, but they keep very late hours.

NANA'S BAR

This is where Portimão's young people meet for a beer or a gin and tonic. The atmosphere is relaxed, though there are occasional fancy-dress parties. *Daily 1pm–4am | Rua José Bivar, Praia da Rocha| FB: Nana's Bar*

TEATRO MUNICIPAL DE PORTIMÃO

TEMPO, located in the former city palace Sárrea, is host to all kinds of cultural events: theatre, ballet, chanson, fado, puppet theatre, classical concerts and much more. Live music is also performed in its adjoining *Café Concerto. Largo 1° Dezembro | tel. 2 82 24 26 50| FB*

AROUND PORTIMÃO

6 ALVOR ★

7km west of Portimão / 10 mins by car on the M531

The *Ria de Alvor*, a wonderfully quiet tidal lagoon in an environmentally protected area, serves as a relaxing retreat for people from across the region. Although a number of hotel complexes have sprung up at the edge of the fishing village of Alvor (pop. 6,300), there is still a lovely atmosphere, which is best experienced on a stroll through the village itself.

Make sure you visit the beautiful, 16th-century *Igreja Matriz* and marvel at the church's delicate, Manueline

stone carvings. You'll find plenty of restaurants and bars in the old town, as well as in the *Zona Ribeirinha* with its broad promenade, including the quaint *Adega d'Alvor (daily | Rua Marquês de Pombal 50 | tel. 2 82 45 74 07 | adegadalvor.pt | €€–€€€)* which serves great seafood. From the port, various boat tours depart for the lagoon and out to sea. The *Praia de Alvor* (see p. 83) is one of the best beaches in the area. *F6*

7 FERRAGUDO ★

5km southeast of Portimão / 10 mins by car on the Ponte Velha

The white houses in this small fishing village (pop. 2,000) are spread out over a hill on the banks of the Arade, and serve as a scenic counterpoint to the tower blocks across the water on the Praia da Rocha. Ferragudo has managed to preserve its picturesque charm, despite everything that has

happened around it. The main square of Praça Rainha Dona Leonor, located at sea level on the Rua 25 de Abril and on the *"Cais" (Rua Infante Santo)*, offers a range of pleasant cafés, grill restaurants and bars with live music. Make sure you also climb through the maze of narrow streets and staircases to the *church*, as from here you can take in a wonderful view over Portimão and the river.

If you want to go for a swim, then head for the beautiful beaches of *Praia da Angrinha* and *Praia Grande*, which are separated from each other by the (privately owned) harbour fortress *São João*. From the *Praia do Molhe* you can walk out onto the estuary breakwater, which extends far into the sea. The beautiful lighthouse, *Farol da Ponta do Altar*, which dates back to 1893, offers superb coastal views. The *Caminho dos Promontórios* allows you to walk along the rocky coast on a well-maintained path. If you go the full 6km distance you will end up in Carvoeiro. *F6*

8 LAGOA

10km east of Portimão / 15 mins by car on the N125

Most people who pass through Lagoa, do so while stuck in a traffic jam on the N125 and never realise what little treasures this administrative centre (pop. 7,200) has to offer. You can leave your car in the large car park in front of the *Adega Cooperativa do Algarve* wine cooperative, where you can also buy good local wine. Next, take a stroll through the streets of the village's beautiful and well-preserved historic centre. Most of the buildings date back to the 18th century, such as the Baroque *Igreja Matriz* or the *Convento de São José* (now used as a cultural centre). The small *market hall* at the eastern end of the old town is also

One of the Algarve's most picturesque resorts: Ferragudo

Natural sculptures at Algar Seco

worth a look; and not far from here is the excellent restaurant *Gaspacho & Migas (closed Sun and lunctimes | Rua Francisco LM Veloso, Lote 5, Loja C | tel. 9 66 59 73 20 | gaspachoemigas.com | €€–€€€).* Chef Ivo Braz and his team serve up fresh regional delicacies with a special twist. ⬚ *G6*

INSIDER TIP
Gourmet cooking with local colour

🔟 CARVOEIRO

11km east of Portimão / 20 mins by car

As recently as the late 20th century, fishermen set the tone at "charcoal burners' beach" but for a long time now, tourism has been the main source of income. The population of 2,800 expands to many times that number during the summer, leaving this attractive village with its many bars and cafés and the expansive holiday resorts surrounding it firmly in the hands of holidaymakers. But you need only take a look at the region's sleepy coves with their sandy beaches – especially the glorious 🏖 *Praia da Marinha* – to understand why it's such a popular spot. You can explore the unique coastal landscape and many of the (often deserted) coves on foot via the beautiful paths that run along the cliffs, in particular towards Armação de Pêra. Don't miss a stroll along the wooden boardwalk from Carvoeiro town

INSIDER TIP
A wooden path to a rocky landscape

centre to *Algar Seco* with its bizarre rock formations, caves and towers. It is just 1 km away. Stop off at the pleasant *Boneca Bar (March–Oct, closed Sun | tel. 2 82 35 83 91 | restaurante bonecabar.com | €–€€)* to enjoy a drink with the bright red rocks as a fantastic backdrop. In the centre of Carvoeiro, *Jota Lita (closed Sun and lunchtimes | Estrada do Farol 28 | tel. 9 35 04 54 39 | €€)* delights its guests with seafood creations, as well as lots of veggie options. *▥ G7*

🔟 SAND CITY 👫
12km east of Portimão / 16 mins by car on the N125

Building sandcastles is not just for kids. Every year, artists from around the world come to this site near Lagoa to craft the most unbelievable constructions and landscapes from sand at the world's biggest sand sculpture festival. From June to September, the figures are illuminated at night, which creates a wonderful atmosphere. *April–Oct | admission 11.90 euros, children aged 6 to 12 years 5.90 euros, 🐷 20% discount online | sandcity.pt | ⏱ 1 hr | ▥ G6*

INSIDER TIP
Sand world under the stars

ALBUFEIRA

(▥ J7) **At first glance, this former fishing village may appear to be an unappealing and built-up holiday resort – especially at the height of the summer when thousands of** tourists descend on the town to take advantage of its vibrant nightlife. However, over time you may well come to love ⭐ Albufeira, thanks to the fantastic beaches both in the middle of town and in the adjacent area.

As a holiday destination, Albufeira (pop. 28,650) has a few unbeatable advantages over other towns. Its central location at the heart of the Algarve makes it a superb starting point for day trips in every direction. What's more, the large selection of cafés and shops in the town centre are a genuine bonus for those who like to wander and browse or sit and relax in a lively resort. And then there's "The Strip – a legendary street full of bars and clubs that is a byword for lively nightlife on the Algarve. In other words, it is a great place to party – as long as you are not put off by the many stag and hen dos. Despite all the crowds, it is still possible to find a few quiet corners in Albufeira among the picturesque streets of the historic *Praia do Peneco* quarter high above the beach, or in the small *Parque de Vale Faro*, northeast of the *Praia do Inatel*.

SIGHTSEEING

In the historic heart of the town perched high above the beach, it is still possible to find a few faint traces of the era of Moorish rule, from which the name Albufeira is derived ("al-buhera" – the lagoon). This hilltop location was once the site of a fortress that defended the settlement. The Rua da Bateria runs along the edge of a cliff and offers superb views over the beaches and the rocky coast, while the tiny *Misericórdia chapel* boasts a Gothic doorway that survived the 1755 earthquake. Housed inside the former town hall, the *Museu Municipal de Arqueologia (closed Mon | admission 1.10 euros | Praça da República 1)* displays artefacts from the Roman and Moorish eras.

Still up for some history? To the west of the main pedestrian street, Rua 5 de Outubro, you can visit three beautiful churches: the 18th-century *Igreja Matriz* parish church; the small *Igreja de São Sebastião*, which features a Manueline side door and is now used as a museum *(Museu de Arte Sacra | closed Mon | admission 2 euros)*, and the Baroque *Igreja de Sant'Ana*. The *Miradouro Pau da Bandeira* to the east of the *Praia dos Pescadores* offers great views over Albufeira, with an escalator taking you to the top.

EATING & DRINKING

THE HOUSE OF STEWS

Don't be put off by the English name (it's rather misleading!). This place is brimming with top-notch, slow-cooked Portuguese cuisine, just like grandma used to make! You can sit in a romantic nook in the dining room with its understated decor or (even better!) in the beautiful outdoor seating area. The menu is just the right (short) length, and you can't go wrong with any of the lovingly prepared stews on offer. Plus, the staff are

Great beaches, vibrant nightlife, central location – welcome to Albufeira!

engaged and friendly and you get good value for money. *Closed Sun and lunchtimes. | Rua Almeida Garret 41A | tel. 9 25 71 27 38 | FB | €€*

UZONJ

You might be left wondering how such a cool and fashionable venue can be so reasonably priced! You can eat a three-course meal at this grill restaurant for around 13 euros, and yet no expense is spared when it comes to culinary refinement or friendly staff. *Closed Wed | Rua Dunfermline | tel. 9 17 84 76 21 | FB: uzonjrestaurante grill | €*

VILA JOYA

If you want to eat somewhere seriously refined and with incredible sea views, then treat yourself to an evening at this two-Michelin-starred gourmet restaurant run by Austrian chef Dieter Koschina. You'll go home raving about it! *Closed Nov–Feb, otherwise daily | Estrada da Galé | tel. 2 89 59 17 95 | vilajoya.com | €€€*

SHOPPING

The alleyways around the pedestrianised streets of Rua 5 de Outubro, Rua Cândido dos Reis and Largo Cais Herculano are full of shops offering all kinds of cheap tourist tat and knock-off clothes, but buried among them are some great craft shops. Albufeira's covered market *(Mercado Municipal dos Caliços | Largo do Mercado)*, on the way out of town to the east, just after the large Lidl store, sells delicious fresh produce from local farmers and fishermen. There is also a flea market here on the second and third Saturdays of the month.

On the roads into Albufeira you will see lots of  locals selling produce from their gardens. You are unlikely to taste such juicy oranges and melons anywhere else – and certainly not at these low prices!

BEACHES

There is no shortage of great beaches in and around Albufeira. Most holidaymakers frequent the two town beaches *Praia dos Pescadores* (near the Cais Herculano) and *Praia do Peneco* (accessed through the beach tunnel on the Rua 5 de Outubro or the lift from the Rua Latino Coelho). East of the town, the long, beautiful

🏴 🦅 *Praia da Falésia* with its shimmering red cliffs (near Olhos de Água) stands out from the rest of the competition. In the evening, as the sun descends, the rock here takes on such a kaleidoscope of colour that a camera is every bit as important as a swimming costume for a day at the beach. Olhos de Água has a unique coastal attraction of its own, which gives the town its name. At low tide, pools of freshwater appear between the algae-covered rocks on the left side of the bay. This rare natural phenomenon is caused by springs bubbling to the surface. According to centuries of fishermen's legends, the springs are a sign that a woman drowned here and continues to cry in perpetuity.

INSIDER TIP
Eyes of water

Located west of Albufeira are pretty little beach coves with friendly beach bars, such as the *praias de São Rafael*, *do Castelo* or *do Evaristo*. The *Praia da Galé* stretches for several kilometres to Salgados and is easy to get to despite its stunning location at the foot of impressive cliffs.

SPORT & ACTIVITIES

Lots of boat trips along the coast set off from the colourful marina to the west of Albufeira, including some 🐵 dolphin-watching tours, such as *Dolphins Driven (April–Oct | 40 euros, children aged 5 to 12 years 25 euros | dolphins.pt)*. On the *Praia dos Pescadores* you can have a go on a banana boat (other inflatables are available) and foot volley

tournaments are also regularly held here. The *Praia da Galé* is great for windsurfing.

The waterslide park 🐵 *Aqualand (June 10am–5pm, July–Sept 10am–6pm | admission 31 euros, children aged 5 to 10 years 22 euros, 🐷 online discount | on the N125 | aqualand.pt)* near Alcantarilha offers all the water-based fun you would wish for. The large zoo and theme park 🐵 *Zoomarine (March–Nov, opening times vary, see website | admission 30–37 euros , children up to 10 years 20–27 euros, children under 1m free, 🐷 10% discount online | near Guia, on the N125 | zoomarine.pt)* has a regular programme of falconry and dolphin displays, but there are also plenty of opportunities to jump in and cool off.

Both little and large climbing nuts will have a great time at the 🐵 *Parque Aventura (opening times vary, see website | Estrada de Santa Eulália | parqueaventura.net)* high-rope course. There are lots of routes for the "curious" *(from 1m, 12 euros)*, "adventurous" *(from 1.30m, 16 euros)* and the "fearless" *(from 1.40m, 20 euros)* to chart their own course through the treetops.

WELLNESS

Do you need a proper massage or a lengthy soak in a luxurious jacuzzi? Then treat yourself to a spa session at the *Hotel Epic Sana (Pinhal do Concelho, Praia da Falésia, Olhos de Água | algarve.epic.sanahotels.com)*. The hotel has one of the best spas on the Algarve, and you do not have to be a guest to book a treatment.

A musical performance in Albufeira's old town

NIGHTLIFE

At night, Albufeira centre gets lively, especially in the vicinity of the *Largo Duarte Pacheco* and along *Rua Cândido dos Reis*. The bar scene is international, but Brits predominate. Live music blares from countless (often Irish) pubs. The (Portuguese) *Bar Sal Rosa (Praça Miguel Bombarda 2 | Tue–Sun 4pm–midnight | tel. 9 27 21 31 16 | FB: barSalRosa),* in the old town, serves delicious cocktails accompanied by great sea views.

The nightlife centre known as "The Strip" is actually *Avenida Sá Carneiro* in the Areias de São João district near the Praia da Oura. Here, bars stand side by side offering something for everyone; the party really gets started after midnight. New bars open on and behind The Strip all the time – explore to your heart's content all the way through to sunrise.

AROUND ALBUFEIRA

11 LAGOA DOS SALGADOS

8km west of Albufeira / 15 mins by car on the Estrada das Sesmarias
Drive through the VidaMar resort to reach the car park at Lagoa dos Salgados. From here, a beautiful footpath follows the banks of the lagoon, which stretches out behind the extensive dunes of the Praia dos Salgados.

This lagoon landscape is both a home and a seasonal stop-over for lots of bird species, and is the perfect spot for birdwatching. The flamingos put on a particularly good show! Paths run west from here all the way to the Praia Grande at Armação de Pêra; heading east, you can walk through the dunes and along the coast as far as Praia da Galé. *H7*

12 ARMAÇÃO DE PÊRA

13km west of Albufeira / 20 mins by car on the M526

Although ugly hotels and apartment blocks have turned this village (pop. 6,000) into a concrete jungle, there are places where it has retained its charm as a former fishing village: at the eastern end of town, for example, where colourful fishing boats moor on the beach, or in the narrow lanes near the white *St Anthony's chapel* and the former *harbour fort*.

The waterfront has a promenade and a 👥 long, wide, sandy beach, which is especially popular with families. There are lots of bars and restaurants near the beach.

As you explore, cast a glance at the casino built in 1936 in a perfect location on the coast. It has been empty and unused since the Carnation Revolution, but is finally having new life breathed into it. *H7*

13 NOSSA SENHORA DA ROCHA ★

16km west of Albufeira / 25 mins by car on the M 26/N269-1

In Alporchinhos, on the western edge of Armação de Pêra, a striking pilgrim's chapel perches on the

clifftop with sweeping views of the coastline. It was built by fishermen in the 16th century, but you could be forgiven for thinking they were trying to attract social media followers even then – the combination of sea, cliffs and white chapel is so perfect that, if you add a sunset, it can all seem a bit too good to be true! Pillars from the sixth or seventh centuries are a Visigoth testimony to early Christianity in the Algarve.

Brought your swimming stuff? At the foot of the 30m-high cliffs, there are beautiful, inviting beaches. And, if you are the walking type, this stretch of coast, as far as *Carvoeiro*, is unrivalled for the variety of its caves, rock formations and secluded coves,

Nossa Senhora da Rocha offers a fantastic colour spectacle for budding photographers

as well as grottoes and arches formed from eroded caves – known as *algares*. *H7*

ALCANTARILHA

10km northwest of Albufeira / 20 mins by car on the M526

This village will be popular with fans of gruesome and spooky sights: the *Capela dos Ossos* next to the village church was built in the 16th century out of thousands of bones. The 1,500 skeletons needed to put the building together came from a discarded cemetery which the new settlement wanted to turn into agricultural land.

Need something to help recover from the chapel? A little way outside the village you can get to know Dona Edite and her superb wines. Dona Edite took over the winery

INSIDER TIP Fine wine

Quinta João Clara (guided tour with tasting by appointment Mon–Fri 11am and 3pm | Vale de Lousas | tel. 9 67 01 24 44 | joaoclara.com) after the death of her husband, and manages it so successfully that she has won lots of awards for her red, white and rosé wines. *H6*

GUIA

7km northwest of Albufeira / 10 mins by car on the M526-1

People from across the Algarve make pilgrimages to the unassuming village of Guia (pop. 4,800). There are three reasons for this. The first is

Almond trees blooming in Paderne in the early spring

Zoomarine (see p. 90), a huge zoo and theme park that attracts hundreds of visitors every day. The second reason is culinary: Guia is a mecca for fans of the most famous grilled chicken in Portugal. Virtually everyone here sells *frango piri-piri*, the spicy barbecue chicken, but it is particularly tasty at *Ramires (daily, no reservations July and Aug | Rua 5 de Abril 14 | tel. 2 89 56 12 32 | restauranteramires. com | €)*, which has been honing its craft since 1964. The third reason to come here is *Algarve Shopping (daily | N125 | algarveshopping.pt)*, a massive shopping mall with cinemas, dozens of shops, supermarkets and fast-food outlets. *J6*

16 PADERNE

12km north of Albufeira / 20 mins by car on the N395

Fancy a quick trip into Moorish history? It is virtually impossible to miss the 12th-century hill fort of *Castelo de Paderne*. Not only is it right by the motorway, but it also stands in a picturesque landscape next to the little Ribeira da Quarteira. However, the ruins are not easy to reach and visit; currently, the access road is in need of repair and they can only be viewed from the outside. All that is left of the old village of Paderne is a patch of rubble near the castle, as it was destroyed during the earthquake in 1755; the inhabitants resettled around 5km to the north. Close to modern Paderne you can go on an oenological and gastronomic discovery tour at *Veneza (closed Tue, open evening only apart from Fri and Sun | tel. 2 89 36 71 29 | restauranteveneza. com | €€–€€€)*, a gourmet restaurant with a well-stacked wine cellar. It offers many excellent meat dishes as well as delicious desserts made with almonds, figs and carob. ▱ *K6*

17 VILAMOURA ★

18km east of Albufeira / 30 mins by car on the M526

The twin villages of Vilamoura-Quarteira (pop. 24,400) make an unusual pair: the beachfront settlement of Quarteira (now disfigured by concrete tower blocks built in the 1970s) grew from an actual village and, as such, has a parish church and a lively *mercado municipal* with an attractive fish hall. Vilamoura, on the other hand, was designed completely from scratch as a tailor-made holiday resort for wealthy visitors … with its own casino, of course. What makes Vilamoura so interesting is how artificial it is – from the casino and the crazily expensive yachts in the harbour to the sports cars on every corner, there is nothing here to remind you of life before high-end tourism. The harbour is lined with elegant bars and restaurants, and is the place on the Algarve where you are most likely to run into a Portuguese celebrity.

If the decadence of the present day gets too much, head to the west of the marina where you can step back in time by visiting the *Cerro da Vila (daily 9.30am–12.30pm and 2–6pm |*

admission 4 euros), a large archaeological site and museum based around a Roman villa from the third century, where (among other things) fish salting took place. The mosaics are amazingly well preserved! ▱ *K7*

THE WEST COAST

WIND, WAVES & WILDERNESS

In the Algarve's wild west you will find untouched landscapes such as the romantic and picturesque Costa Vicentina – a unique, isolated and sometimes rather hostile rocky coast where the wind whips through your hair and the waves are more suited to surfing than swimming.

The entire length of the Costa Vicentina is a protected nature reserve, and a wonderful long-distance trail runs all along this spectacular coast. The cliffs are interrupted here and there by valleys

Walkers and surfers are drawn to the natural beauty of the Costa Vicentina

where rivers have worn clefts in the rock; the resulting estuary lagoons open out onto wonderfully scenic beaches that are seldom crowded. The area is a little too raw for mass tourism; it appeals more to independent travellers clad in windcheaters.

It's well worth experiencing the magic of Europe's wild and romantic southwestern corner, even if it's only on a day trip – but if you have the time and the inclination, then this amazing landscape is ripe for exploring on foot.

THE WEST COAST

MARCO POLO HIGHLIGHTS

★ **SAGRES**
This harbour town has a fortress and
sheltered beaches ➤ p. 100

★ **CABO DE SÃO VICENTE**
Europe's most southwesterly point is
swept by wind and waves ➤ p. 103

★ **ARRIFANA**
There's a spectacular view of the
crescent-shaped bay and the steep rocky
coast ➤ p. 108

Praia de Odeceixe

Odeceixe **5**

120

Rogil

Praia Amoreira

✓ **6**

Aljezur
p. 104

120

6 **Arrifana** ★

✓ **1**

If you love to ride
the waves, then the
area around Aljezur
and Carrapateira is
perfect for you; there
are surf camps for
beginners here too.

65 km, 1 hr 10 mins

Bordeira

7 Carrapateira
Praia do Amado
✓ **1**

4 Pedralva

Barão de São João

268

Barão de São Miguel

Budens

Vila do Bispo **2**

3

Nossa Senhora de Guadalupe

Bring a jacket with
you! If you take a day
trip from warmer
climes to windswept
Sagres, you might find
yourself shivering in
your light summer
clothes. But you might
also like to buy a
woolly jumper at Cabo
São Vicente …

Praia do Beliche

Cabo de São Vicente **1**
5 ✓

1 **Sagres** ★
p. 100

O C E A N O

PORTUGAL BEJA

266

Pereiras

MARCO POLO BUCKET LIST

1 ✓ Ride the perfect wave

The best spots for *surfing* (or learning to surf) are on the west coast beaches ➤ p. 102, p. 108, p. 109

5 ✓ Salute the sun

The best sunset can be found at the windswept *Cabo de São Vicente* ➤ p. 103

6 ✓ Take a donkey along the coast

Your long-eared friend will carry your luggage while you enjoy the views of *Aljezur* ➤ p. 106

A hiker's paradise: whether you're tackling the epic Rota Vicentina or following one of the many circular routes – the best corners of the west coast can be discovered on foot.

Marmelete

267

You will need a car to explore the length of the west coast; the bus will only take you to the villages, but not to the fantastic beaches.

266

FARO

Albufeira de Odeáxere

43 km · 40 mins

Moinhos Velhos

Silves

A22

Bensafrim

Mexilhoeira Grande

Estômbar

Odiáxere

Parchal

Lagoa

Monte Judeu

Alvor

Portimão

Ferragudo

Lagos

Carvoeiro

Luz

Deep in the west … it gets wilder, windier and quieter; no beds fit for a king, no hustle and bustle, but lots of smaller spots and plenty of nature. Most accommodation options and places to eat can be found in Sagres.

If you choose Sagres as your base, bear in mind that it's quite a long journey (1½ hrs) from Faro airport! The motorway ends in Lagos. The same goes for excursions to the eastern Algarve or the Serra de Monchique.

▲

4 km
2.49 mi

A T L Â N T I C O

SAGRES

(🗺 B8) **In days gone by, this place was thought to be the end of the world – so it's little wonder that the southwesternmost point of continental Europe projects an air of mystery and adventure.**

⭐ Sagres is still associated with 15th-century Portugal's spirit of discovery. However, even before then it served as a place of worship for the Moors and the Romans, and it was the latter who gave the area its name: *Promontorium Sacrum*, or "sacred headland". Today, Sagres is not just the name of the country's most southwesterly point but also that of a well-known brand of Portuguese beer (although the beer is brewed in Lisbon).

Sagres (pop. 1,900) has changed a lot in recent years thanks to its most important resource: the seemingly endless stream of perfect surf that hits its shores. This has led to an explosion of hostels, surf camps and relaxed cafés in this otherwise bland town. It is hard to pinpoint a proper town centre, but the busiest spots are around the Praça da República and along the Rua Comandante Matoso – and of course, the stunningly beautiful beaches that all face in different directions, so that at least one of them will be sheltered from the wind on any given day.

SIGHTSEEING

FORTALEZA DE SAGRES
This rather over-zealously restored 17th-century fortress bars the way to the *Ponta de Sagres*, a barren rocky plateau that extends for a considerable distance into the turbulent sea. This is where Henry the Navigator stood in the 15th century and dreamed of striking out for new lands – he may also have gathered scholars here to discuss and develop his plans. His dreams of discovery became reality thanks, in part, to new navigational techniques and the introduction of the more manoeuvrable caravel ship design. Within two generations, an insignificant region on the edge of Europe had become a wealthy seafaring nation.

The role played by Sagres's famous *rosa dos ventos* ("rose of the winds") in these developments will likely never be known. Discovered here in 1928, it consists of a paved circle, 43m across, marked out into segments that suggest it may have been used as a giant compass or a sundial. It is the first thing you see when you enter through the impregnable walls of the fortress. The only other original building is the small *Nossa Senhora da Graça* chapel, everything else here being a more modern addition. Ignore these recent eyesores apart from the one that houses an interesting, state-of-the-art exhibition on Portuguese expansion, and go for a stroll around the spit of land they are built on, as the real highlight here is the view from the top of the 60m-high cliffs. *Daily 9.30am–5.30pm, until 8pm in summer | admission 3 euros | ⏱ 1½ hrs*

PORTO DA BALEEIRA 🚩
It's worth making a detour down to the fishing port nestled at the eastern

![Porto da Baleeira: proof that some Algarvians still depend on fishing for their livelihood]

Porto da Baleeira: proof that some Algarvians still depend on fishing for their livelihood

end of Sagres, where a few Algarvios still make their living from the fishing industry. Time your visit to coincide with the return of the colourful boats into the harbour, fully laden with fish. The action every afternoon at the *auction hall (Mon–Fri 7.30–10am and 3.30–8pm)* is very entertaining. Traders and chefs come from far and wide to bid on the valuable seafood, as the fish auction in Sagres is reputed to be one of the best in Europe.

EATING & DRINKING

A SEREIA

You won't find fresher fish anywhere.

INSIDER TIP
The freshest fish on the Algarve

Located above the auction room in Sagres's port, you will likely be surrounded by real fishermen as you tuck in to your lunch. *Mon–Fri*

8am–7pm | Porto de Pesca da Baleeira | tel. 2 82 10 96 82 | FB: asereiasagres | €–€€

BAHARI

It's not just windsurfers who love this wonderful bar on Martinhal beach. There is always fresh fish and seafood, but the best thing is the sunset. *Closed Mon in winter | tel. 9 18 61 34 10 | IG: @baharibeachsagres | €€*

ESTRELA DO MAR

This basic, down-to-earth place is a popular meeting spot for locals as well as tourists. It serves fish specialities, wine and beer. *Daily | Rua Comandante Matoso | tel. 2 82 62 40 65 | €*

VILA VELHA

This top-quality restaurant is elegant and relaxed. The high standard of its cuisine has made it one of the most

Surfers at Praia do Tonel wait for the perfect wave

popular places to eat in Sagres; you'll find refined fish and meat dishes as well as more unusual dishes such as rabbit or lamb, and attentive waiters will serve you the perfect wine to accompany your fine meal. *Closed Mon and Wed (and Thu June–Oct) | Rua António Patrão Faustino | tel. 2 82 62 47 88 | vilavelha-sagres.com | €€–€€€*

BEACHES

While the *Praia da Mareta* beach, located in the middle of Sagres, is largely sheltered from the westerly winds, big waves that are perfect for surfing roll into shore to the west of the *ponta* at *Praia do Tonel* and *Praia do Beliche*. The latter is tucked under high cliffs and only accessible down a long wooden stairway. The *Praia do Martinhal* behind the fishing port is popular with windsurfers, and the offshore islands here are a sanctuary for birdlife. Around 15km east of Sagres lie the stunning rocky coves *Praia do Zavial* and *Praia da Ingrina*, which can be reached by car via Raposeira.

SPORT & ACTIVITIES

There are a number of ✅ surf schools on this wave-riding riviera, including the *Freeride Surf Camp (frsurf.com)*. The sea around Sagres not only has the best waves in Portugal, it also has some of the richest fish stocks, making the region a paradise for scuba divers – contact the *Divers Cape diving school (diverscape.net)*. Speaking of wildlife: you can go on dolphin-watching tours with 👥 *Marilimitado (marilimitado.*

com) or time your visit to attend the *birdwatching festival (birdwatchingsagres.com)* during the peak migration season at the start of October.

There are also two great long-distance trails for hikers, the *Via Algarviana (viaalgarviana.org)* and the *Rota Vicentina (rotavicentina.com)* both of which end at Cabo de São Vicente. The 10km section of the Rota Vicentina that runs from the cape to the *Torre de Aspa* – the highest point on this coast at 156m – is breathtakingly beautiful yet surprisingly neglected by tourists.

AROUND SAGRES

1 CABO DE SÃO VICENTE ⭐

6km west of Sagres / 8 mins by car on the N268

An enormous lighthouse marks the most southwesterly point in continental Europe, where 70m cliffs hold back the wind and waves. The cape is the most-visited destination on the Algarve, but the crowds tend to gather at the food and souvenir stands in the car park during the day. If you walk a short way along the cliffs to the north or east (taking extreme care, especially when it's windy!) or arrive at ✅ sunset, you can enjoy the magnificent scenery in peace.

The lighthouse, built in 1904, is no longer open to visitors but the surrounding complex , which was built in 1846, is impressive from the outside.

The lighthouse is visible from 90km away thanks to its 3,000-watt lamps, making it among the most powerful in Europe.

A *hot dog stand (March–Oct daily approx. 10.30am–5.30pm)* here has become famous far beyond the western Algarve because it sells genuine bratwurst imported directly from Germany, freshly grilled on the spot and served with a certificate confirming that you have just consumed the last bratwurst available on this side of the Atlantic. *B7*

2 VILA DO BISPO

10km (6 miles) north of Sagres / 10 mins by car on the N268

The main landmark in this inland resort (pop. 950) is the old *water tower* perched at the town's highest point. The focal points of community life are the market building and the cafés lining the church square; beyond that the place is rather sleepy. However, the nearby beaches *Praia do Castelejo* and *Praia da Cordoama* are glorious and rarely crowded, even in summer.

Perhaps even more beautiful is the hiking trail that leads all the way to the Cabo de São Vicente, 13km from Vila do Bispo along the clifftops – it's simply spectacular! *B–C7*

3 NOSSA SENHORA DE GUADALUPE

14km east of Sagres / 15 mins by car on the N268 / N125

On the N125 just after Raposeira, you will come across this unassuming white chapel – which is a rarity, as it is believed to have been built shortly

Whitewashed houses cluster below the castle ruins in Aljezur

after the expulsion of the Moors in the 13th century, making it one of the oldest churches on the Algarve. It boasts many beautiful Romanesque and Gothic elements, from the small rose window to its keystones and capitals. *Tue–Sun 10am–1pm and 2–6pm, Oct–Apr 9am–1pm and 2–5pm | admission 2 euros | ☐ C7*

◢ PEDRALVA

20km north of Sagres / 20 mins by car on the N268

This once almost-abandoned village has experienced a renaissance thanks to tourism, and its houses have been renovated and can now be rented as traditional-style holiday homes. Even if you're not staying here, it's worth poking around the picturesque alleyways, especially as you might find yourself at *Pizza Pazza (closed Mon, evening only Tue and Sat | tel. 2 82 63 91 73 | IG: @pizzapazzapedralva | €–€€)* which serves the best pizzas for miles around (book in advance!). ☐ *C6*

ALJEZUR

(☐ D4) **It's easy to fall in love with Aljezur, which – with a population of 3,450 – is the biggest place in a very sparsely populated area. The village-sized town is so homely and welcoming that you'll want to start exploring straight away – climbing its steep, picturesque streets lined with whitewashed houses and then heading on to the ruins of its Moorish castle and the small, enchanting market hall by the river.**

It won't take you long to work out why so many people from other countries have moved to the area, especially when you realise how close it is to some stunning coves and beaches.

SIGHTSEEING

MUSEUMS

You will come across several museums as you walk up to the castle through the old town. The small *Museu de Arte Sacra (Rua São João de Deus)* next to the 16th-century *Igreja da Misericórdia* has a collection of religious exhibits, while the *Museu Municipal (Largo 5 de Outubro)* is housed in the 19th-century former town hall. One interesting room here is devoted to relics from the era of Muslim rule in the Middle Ages, while another contains an archaeological exhibition. Upstairs is an anthropological exhibition. 🐖 For just 2.20 euros you can visit every museum in town – including the *Museu Antoniano* inside the former chapel of St Anthony, with its collection of contemporary church art, and the *Casa-Museu Pintor José Cercas*, , once the home of the 20th-century Portuguese artist.. *All museums:*

Tue–Sat 9am–1pm and 2–5pm (until 6pm in summer)

CASTELO 🐖

Perched at the top of the hill, with stunning views down to the Ribeira de Aljezur, is the ruin of a Moorish castle which is free to visit. It has never been extensively restored and as a result blends even more imperceptibly into the landscape. It is a short ten-minute climb to get there (a little strenuous in the heat of the summer), but it's well worth every step for the stunning panoramic view over the green hills stretching to the Serra de Monchique on one side and the sea on the other. Information panels tell the story of this castle from the 10th century and how the Christian crusaders conquered it in the 13th century. You can also drive up by car, but the walk through the village is more enjoyable.

EATING & DRINKING

BAR LAVAR

A traveller's dream: laundry facilities, remote working, space for the kids to play – all washed down with the best coffee in Aljezur. Plus there are healthy snacks! All you could ask for in a launderette. *Closed Sun | Rua 29 de Agosto, Loja | tel. 962 21 09 24 | barlavar.com | €*

CAFÉ DO MERCADO

Friendly café serving snacks next to the indoor market hall. You can stock up on fresh fruit next door. *Daily | Largo do Mercado | €*

MOAGEM

A huge group of people banded together to lovingly convert this old cornmill into an alternative cultural centre (offering yoga, exhibitions, concerts and much else) and a vegetarian café. The *café (closed Sun/Mon)* in the barn serves delicious coffee and snacks, and the adjoining *Bar À Lareira (Fri evenings only)* features live music starting at 8.30pm. *Closed Sun | Rua João Dias Mendes 13–14 | tel. 9 25 28 90 81 | FB: moagemmoagem | €*

PONT'A PÉ

This cosy restaurant, café and bar is a stone's throw from the river and has become an institution thanks to its

good hearty food, often with the famous local sweet potatoes as a side dish. Try the grilled sardines or the razor clam rice with shrimp! The best seats are on the terrace. *Closed Sun | Largo de Liberdade 12 | tel. 2 82 99 81 04 | pontape.pt | €€*

SPORT & ACTIVITIES

☺ ✅ Donkey-trekking is not just a great holiday experience for kids. German expat Stefanie Maier combines a donkey sanctuary *(Burros & Artes | tel 9 63 88 00 53 | burrosartes. com)* with a donkey-trekking business, giving the animals their necessary exercise. The treks take in the Aljezur countryside and coast *(dates and prices on request)*. It's sometimes unclear who is leading whom, but the good-tempered animals are carrying your bags, so perhaps they have the right to choose which way to go. The treks are so enjoyable that they sometimes lead to lifelong friendships developing between those who have taken part. Burros & Artes also offers fantastic pottery workshops.

BEACHES

There are a lot of gorgeous bays near Aljezur. The sea can get pretty rough around here, which means surfers tend to like this stretch of coast more than swimmers. That said, the scenery is so stunning that a day at the beach here has its own charm – you will find it hard to track down a more romantic experience in the Algarve than watching the sun going down over the cliffs above a pretty cove.

The best local *praias* include Amado, Carrapateira, Arrifana, Monte Clérigo and Odeceixe. There is plenty of space at all of these, and they don't even get particularly busy in summer. The best of the bunch, however, is 🏃 *Praia Amoreira*, a 500m stretch of sand that is enclosed by dramatic cliffs to the north (there is a path up to them next to the café). The Ribeira de Aljezur enters the wild Atlantic at the southern edge of the beach, and may prevent you from reaching the beach, depending on the season and tide. It's a perfect spot for windswept walks or watch surfers riding the waves, perhaps from the *Paraiso do Mar* beach bar.

AROUND ALJEZUR

5 ODECEIXE

16km north of Aljezur / 18 mins by car on the N120

This charming village (pop. 1,050), with its inviting street cafés on the Largo 1 de Maio, is located at the northernmost point on the Algarve. From here, you need only cross the Rio Seixe to find yourself in Alentejo, which is well worth a visit; but first, head west, and after 2km you will reach one of the most beautiful beaches in Portugal. The enormous sandy expanse of the *Praia de Odeceixe* is flanked by steep cliffs; the Rio Seixe estuary forms a wonderful lagoon to swim in, and the beachfront cafés serve ice-cold white wine and fresh barnacles *(perceves)*. It's heaven on earth! If you decide to head into the village itself, *Restaurante Chaparro (closed Thu in winter | Rua Estrada National 8 | tel. 2 82 94 73 04 | €€)* is a great spot for excellent seafood.

The pretty streets in the village are a pleasure to stroll around. As you explore, look out for the *Moinho de Odeceixe*, which should be on everyone's itinerary. The *Moinho* is one of numerous windmills that used to operate in this area – proof that this corner of Portugal has never been short of wind! It now operates as a small museum *(June–Sept Tue–Sat 10am–4.30pm | free admission | Serro da Igreja |* ⏱ *15 mins)* and offers a great view of Odeceixe, especially at sunset. 🗺 *D3*

Donkey-trekking is a fun way to explore the area

Golden sand and Atlantic surf at Praia da Bordeira

6 ARRIFANA ⭐

10km southwest of Aljezur / 13 mins by car on the M1003-1

Set on a semi-circular bay, this relaxed town is very popular with ✅ surfers. Head to the ruins of the 17th-century fort on the *Ponta da Arrifana* for magnificent views of crescent-shaped Arrifana bay and the striking coastline. It's the perfect spot for a picnic with a bottle of wine … especially when the sun is going down. If you don't want to take your own food, there is a good restaurant specialising in seafood right in front of the *fortaleza*, with big windows to take in the view: *Restaurante O Paulo (tel. 2 82 99 51 84 | restauranteopaulo.com | €€).* 🗺 *C4*

7 CARRAPATEIRA

20km south of Aljezur / 20 mins by car on the N120/N268

This spot – nestled on the edge of green hills next to enormous, sandy *Praia da Bordeira* – is as endearing as they come. *Carrapateira* is part of the municipality of Bordeira and, taken together, the whitewashed houses of these two villages are home to 370 inhabitants. The small 16th-century *village church* offers great views over the picturesque settlement and its surroundings. Life here centres on the tiny market and the cafés around it. The friendly restaurant *Alecrim (closed Thu | Rua dos Quintais 2 | tel. 9 36 22 05 06 | €)* offers vegetarian and vegan options.

Due to the natural fertility of the soil, traditionally more people in Carrapateira worked the land than the sea, although fishing was (and still is) regarded as an important side-line – which is why the locals are often referred to as "amphibians". You can find out all about their lives and livelihoods through the centuries at the *Museu do Mar e da Terra (Mon–Fri 9am–3.30pm | admission 2.70 euros | Rua do Pescador)*.

The sea still plays a key role here today as you will be able to tell from the many happy surfers who stop in Carrapateira for an invigorating coffee after riding waves on *Praia da Bordeira* and ✅ 🏴 ☀️ *Praia do Amado (🗺 C6)* to the south. Even if you're no surfer yourself, the atmosphere on Amado beach is pretty special: you can sit back and watch the wave-riders for hours!

A stunning section of the *Rota Vicentina* long-distance path passes through here, crossing the breathtakingly beautiful *Ponta de Carrapateira* headland. You'll get the best views of this rocky coastline if you walk between Carrapateira and Praia do Amado rather than driving along the dusty road as most visitors do.

INSIDER TIP
Spectacular cliffs all the way

There are plenty of other signposted hiking trails around Carrapateira and Bordeira, including some routes through the green hinterland. You will find fresh *perceves* – the "goose barnacles" that are so typical of this region – in lots of restaurants around here, but they are particularly good at

Sítio do Rio (closed Mon | Praia da Amado | tel. 2 82 97 39 14 | €). 🗺 *C5–6*

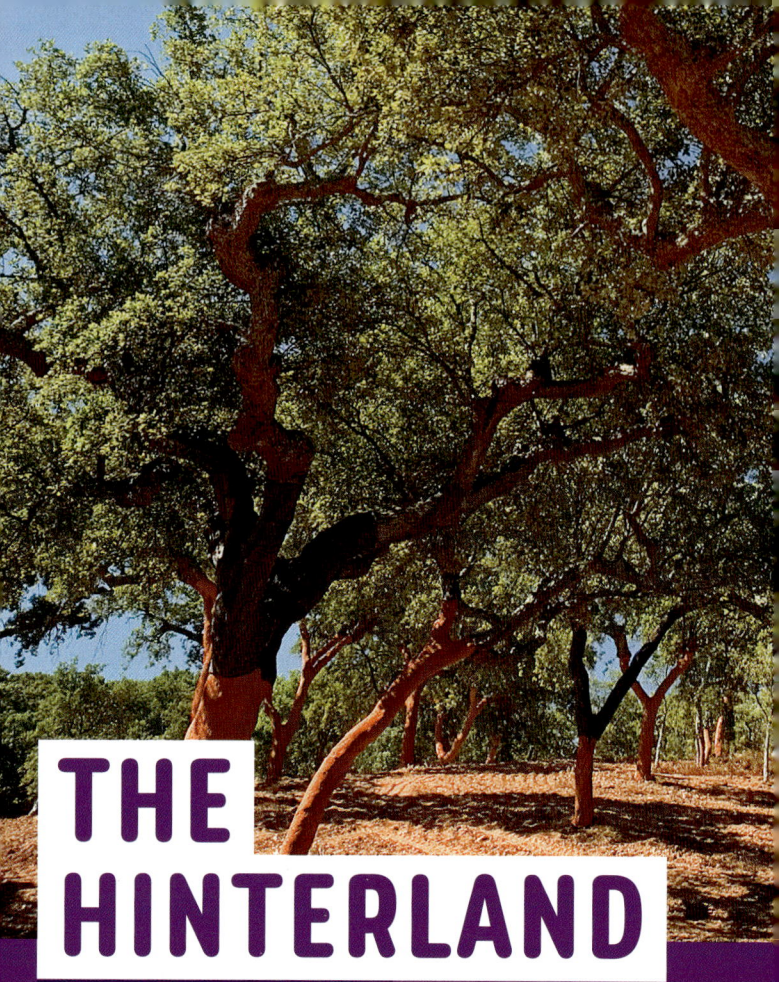

THE HINTERLAND

A DIFFERENT ALGARVE

When visitors think of the Algarve, they don't tend to summon up images of mountains and remote hillside villages, or of fertile valleys and cork plantations. It does not even occur to most holidaymakers to explore the area north of the A22 motorway. However, those that do will discover an altogether different side to the Algarve.

Cork oak forests provide shade in the Serra de Monchique

Even the three major towns here have nothing in common with the hustle and bustle of the coast. They are surrounded by wonderfully peaceful countryside that gives them a sense of remoteness. Rural traditions still characterise the "Garden of the Algarve", as this region is sometimes known. Hiking trails lead through a variety of hot and dry, or humid and fertile landscapes that offer a refreshing contrast to the densely populated areas along the coast.

THE HINTERLAND

Walk in the cork oak forest, beside reservoirs, along the paths of the Via Algarviana or on a plateau: the hinterlands offer a variety of walking routes.

Had enough of sand and sea? Portimão is less than an hour from the summit of Fóia, where you can drink in the mountain air. Make sure you pack a jumper, as it's often much chillier when you're 900m high!

The hinterland makes a great base for holidays too! How about stopping off in Monchique to go hiking or take a trip to the coast?

Silves is a great option for Sunday afternoons: amble through the alleyways, pop into the castle, and then listen to live music at Café Inglês.

Santa Clara-a-Velha

Santana da Serra

BEJA

Barragem de Santa Clara

Pereiras

IC1

266

São Marcos da Serra

267

Alférce

29km, 8 hrs

IC1

Medronho Distillery

8 ✓

2

3 Fóia

✓ **7**

Monchique
p. 117

4 Picota

Serra de Monchique

5 Caldas de Monchique ★

Serra de Monchique ★

São Bartolomeu de Messines

A2

266

Canhestris

Silves ★
p. 114

Tunes

Mexilhoeira Grande

1 Algoz

Portimão

A22

Estômbar

Parchal

Lagoa

125

Porches

Alcantarilha

Guia

Ferreiras

Alvor

Ferragudo

Pêra

Armação de Pêra

Albufeira

Carvoeiro

Local public transport only sporadically visits the villages of the hinterlands, so you're better off in a car.

88km, 1½ hrs

50km, 40 mins

Santa Bárbara de Padrões

Rosário

Rocha da Pena **7**

8 Salir

6 Alte

Benafim

PORTUGAL

São Barnabé

São Bartolomé

124

9 Fonte Benémola

Tôr

Querença

FARO

Paderne

Loulé is pretty sleepy on Sundays; it's best to visit when the covered market is open. The bustling Saturday morning market is particularly lively!

Alportel

São Brás de Alportel **10**

9 ✓

Loulé ★
p. 122

Santa Bárbara de Nexe

Vale Formoso

125

Almancil

A22

4 km
2.49 mi

After visiting the cathedral, enjoy a *galão* next door!

SILVES

(🗺 G5–6) **The tranquil regional country town of ⭐ Silves (pop. 10,600) – formerly known as Xelb and capital of the Moorish province of Al-Gharb – is a great place to track down what is left of the Moors and their rich culture. Or alternatively, just sit back in a café and enjoy the here and now!**

It is hard to imagine now that "Xelb" was once more important than Lisbon, and even comparable to Granada. A few remnants of the era of Moorish rule can be found in the archaeological museum and in the heavily restored castle, which glows bright red in the light of the sun. However, the town has changed a good deal since the Reconquista in the mid-13th century. This is partly due to the 1755 earthquake, but also because its main artery – the Rio Arade, which the Phoenicians once sailed up to access this part of the country, and which was the reason why the Moors established their capital here in the fertile, well-irrigated hinterland – has silted up. During low tide (that's right, the tide comes in all the way up to Silves!), the river is reduced to little more than a stream flowing under the town's beautiful five-arched 15th-century bridge.

Despite all these changes, Silves is a picturesque and charming little town, and it's fun to wander through its streets, climb up to the castle, browse through its shops or sit back in one of its charming cafés.

SIGHTSEEING

CASTELO

It's worth climbing to the top of the impregnable walls of the Moorish fortress (8th–13th centuries) for the wonderful views alone, which take in the rooftops of the town and the surrounding orange groves. You can then walk from tower to tower along the top of the dark-red sandstone walls, which were a little over-zealously restored during the 1940s. Make sure you also head down into the enormous 13th-century cistern (which now houses an interesting exhibition about the Iberian lynx) and take a look at the (unfortunately rather scant) excavations of the Moorish palace.

The cosy *café (€)* in the inner courtyard serves small snacks and delicious fruit juices. *Daily 9am–6pm, May–Sept until 8pm | admission 2.80 euros, combined ticket with the Archaeological Museum 3.90 euros |* ⏱ *1 hr*

MUSEU MUNICIPAL DE ARQUEOLOGIA

Next to the city wall's erstwhile fortified tower, the *Torreão da Porta da Cidade*, you'll find the interesting *Archeological Museum*. Finds dating from the Stone Age through to medieval times are exhibited here, including some beautiful Arabic ceramics. The descent into a 20m-deep Moorish well shaft, around which the museum was built, is spellbinding. *Tue–Sun 10am–6pm | admission 2.10 euros, combined ticket with the castelo 3.90 euros | Rua das Portas de Loulé 14 |* ⏱ *45 mins*

SÉ

Below the castle looms the mid-13th-century cathedral – also built of red sandstone – which like so many churches was constructed on the ruins of the mosque. Despite severe damage during the 1755 earthquake, a few Gothic elements have been preserved, such as on the entrance portal, the choir and the crossing. *Mon–Fri 10am–1pm and 2–5pm | admission 2 euros, covered shoulders required |* ⏱ *20 mins*

EATING & DRINKING

CAFÉ DAROSA

This venerable coffee house in the town hall has been charmingly restored. The blue and white *azulejos* on its walls shine again, and the cakes are superb – the chocolate one is the pick of the bunch.

INSIDER TIP
Coffee, cake and dazzling tiles

Outside, the tables are in a beautiful arcade. *Closed Sun | Largo do Município 6 | tel. 2 82 14 80 34 | FB: CafeDaRosa | €*

CAFÉ INGLÊS

Enjoy a pizza, a salad or a slice of home-made cake in this lovely café. On Friday and Saturday evenings, as well as Sunday afternoons, you even get a side of live music. *Closed Mon | Rua do Castelo 11 | tel. 2 82 44 25 85 | cafeingles.com.pt | €€*

O BARRADAS

Andrea Pequeno is a master chef while her husband Luís is a charming front of house expert. Their restaurant is a must if you want to have a delicious and elegant dinner in the Silves area. Try their fish baked in salt! *Evenings only, closed Wed | Venda Nova (2km to the south) | tel. 9 61 65 73 57 | obarradas.com | €€*

RESTAURANTE-BISTRO RAINHA

The "Queen" really leaves nothing to be desired: beautifully prepared dishes at fair prices, a convivial atmosphere, and a picturesque location on the Rio Arade, around 8km northwest of Silves (in the direction of the Arade dam). The trip is so worth it! *Sun only lunchtime, Wed–Sat only evenings, sometimes closed Mon/Tue in winter | Santo Estévão/Barragem de Silves | tel. 9 15 23 36 36 | FB: restauranterainha. algarve | €€*

SPORT & ACTIVITIES

If you want to travel to Silves by boat up the *Rio Arade* – just like the Phoenicians did – then you can set sail for a 4½-hr trip (with a 1½-hr stop in Silves) on the solar-powered "sunboat" *(departure times depend on the tides | 39 euros, children aged 3 to 10 years 25 euros) | algarvesunboat.com)* from the marina in Portimão. There is also some great hiking by the *Barragem do Funcho* reservoir, 18km to the northeast of Silves. Near Algoz (see p. 117) *Krazy World petting zoo (daily 10am–6pm, in summer until 6.30pm, in winter until 5.30pm | admission*

Fóia, the highest peak in the Algarve, provides the best views

16.95 euros, children aged 4 to 10 years 9.95 euros | krazyworld.com) mainly attracts young families. The most entertaining animals are definitely the lemurs, who splash around on the water slides!

AROUND SILVES

🟥1 ALGOZ

14km (8.5 miles) east of SIlves / 15 mins by car on the N269

At first, this tranquil provincial village – tucked away from the hustle and bustle – does not seem to have much to write home about. However, nearby on the road to Ferreiras you will find *Quinta dos Avós (Tue–Sat 10am–12.30pm and 2–6pm | IG: @Quintadosavos.pt)*, a pastry shop with bakery attached which specialises in traditional medieval monastic desserts. 📖 *J6*

MONCHIQUE

(📖 F4) **Looking for some clear mountain air? Then head for the ⭐ Serra de Monchique, and make sure you take your walking boots with you! From the coastal villages around Portimão, it takes less than an hour to get to the highest peak in the Algarve, the 902m Mount Fóia. The mountain town of Monchique is also well worth a visit.**

Monchique (pop. 4,800) has the atmosphere of a small village and is located around 460m up in the "groove" between the two main peaks of the mountain range. Its small streets run uphill, and its many cafés, bars and restaurants are good places to take a well-earned break if you have been exploring the *serra* on foot. A lot of day-trippers just head to the summit of *Mount Fóia*, which offers some magnificent views on sunny days but is also spoilt by some aesthetically unappealing telecommunication masts.

The real appeal of the mountains will become apparent if you hike through cork oak forests to the top of *Picota* (773m), explore the area on a mountain bike, or get to know the region's flora on foot. The coastal mountains are blessed with over 1,000 different plant species. The *serra* is particularly worth visiting in spring, when the rock roses, wild orchids, camellias, azaleas and rhododendrons come into bloom. Sadly, however, this garden of the Algarve is repeatedly destroyed by devastating forest fires.

You can also gain an impression of the landscape from your car. One particularly appealing drive runs down the N267 from Monchique to São Marcos da Serra, via Alferce, where you can take a beautiful hike over the Passadiço do Barranco do Demo, a cool stairway with a suspension bridge! Alternatively, if you come from the south, there is a great route through the Ribeira de Odelouca's fertile valley: head out from Porto Lagos on the N124 towards Silves, then turn left towards Barragem de Odelouca to eventually reach *Alferce (ṁ G4)*.

En route, make sure you stop off at the *Barragem de Odelouca*, which is a great spot for a picnic. The reservoir here is one of the main water sources for the whole region.

On the subject of water – the volcanic geology around Monchique means there are a lot of 🍃 natural springs (*fontes*) producing fresh drinking water. Do as the locals do and fill your bottles up whenever you see one!

SIGHTSEEING

IGREJA MATRIZ

This village church from the 15th and 16th centuries is in daily use by the reverent residents of Monchique. However, while the tourists who visit come to see its extraordinary portal, which is surrounded by a twisted stone arc ending in massive knots (a typical feature of Manueline architecture). The chestnut-wood altar has a statue of *Nossa Senhora da Conceição* dating from the 18th century.

NOSSA SENHORA DO DESTERRO

A short, well-signposted footpath starting in the town square (Largo dos Chorões) leads out through the narrow streets and into a cork oak forest to reach this Franciscan monastery, which was founded in 1631. There's not much left, since it was destroyed in the 1755 earthquake and then abandoned, but there are beautiful views from here over Monchique.

EATING & DRINKING

As you drive up to the top of Mount Fóia, you will pass a few rustic eateries that offer a good opportunity to stop for a break. It's also worth visiting the hilltop restaurant *Jardim das Oliveiras (closed Sun eve and Tue | Sítio do Porto Escuro | tel. 2 82 91 28 74 | jardimdasoliveiras.com | €€)*, which is signposted on the road up to Fóia. Surrounded by olive groves, this restaurant has lots of outdoor seating and is famous for its hearty sausage and meat dishes (even wild boar). Monchique itself also boasts a number of good restaurants.

A CHARRETTE

Extremely relaxed with bags of ambiance and rustic charm. Wild boar, lamb stew, black pig and other *serra* specialities. The menu is only available in Portuguese, but that can be an adventure in itself and good wines might help, too. *Closed Wed | Rua Dr Samora Gil 30–34 | next to the town hall | tel. 2 82 91 21 42 | €€*

ÓCHÃLÁ

Head up the small pedestrianised street from the town square, Largo dos Chorões, to reach this friendly teahouse, which also serves delicious home-made pastries, sandwiches, salads and small vegetarian plates. *Closed evenings and Sun (also Sat in winter) | Rua Doutor Samora Gil 12 | tel. 2 82 91 25 24 | €*

Traditional crafts and traditional transport in Monchique

SHOPPING

A variety of quality shops sell ceramics, wooden souvenirs, baskets and leather goods. Folding wooden chairs, unique to the *serra*, are a favourite tourist souvenir from the region (but it requires careful logistical planning to get them home). They are hand-crafted to a design that can be traced back to the Romans, and are believed to be the first ever folding chairs. (The Romans were also making good use of the nearby hot springs at the resort of Caldas 2,000 years ago.) The other thing to track down up here is *medronho*, the locally produced spirit. The best place to get it is the *Loja de Mel e Medronho*, a proper booze shop founded when 50 local producers grouped together to sell their concoctions at a central point (the village square). Make sure to try before you buy – there is a considerable difference between the punchy *medronho* and slightly sweeter *melosa* (which has cinnamon and honey added to it).

SPORT & ACTIVITIES

The *serra* is a beautiful area for hiking and cycling – and a vast one. It has an endless network of roads, paths and trails that cover the Fóia and Picota mountains and the valleys, including the *Via Algarviana* hiking trail, which runs right through it. Cyclists who brave the 902m climb up to Mount Fóia will be rewarded with the thrill of coasting down the 35km route to the sea. Motorists have to be very careful,

The fruit of the strawberry tree is the main ingredient in *medronho*

especially at weekends when there are many cyclists on the road.

✔ You can book a superb guided mountain-bike tour from Mount Fóia to the Ria de Alvor (downhill for most of the route!) with the guys at *Outdoor Tours (outdoor-tours.com)*.

INSIDER TIP
Two-wheel tour

They'll provide the bikes, show you some beautiful spots in the *serra* and even arrange a gloriously traditional lunch in Casais's village café for you.

WELLNESS

There aren't many places in the Algarve where you can wallow in a hot spring, but *Caldas de Monchique* (see p.122) fit the bill. Guests can relax in warm water (32°C) in the spa or enjoy a sauna, Vichy shower and a range of spa and beauty treatments in the surrounding hotels. All the treatments can be booked online through the *Villa Termal Caldas de Monchique Resort (monchiquetermalresort.com)*. Alternatively, the nearby (more modern) Macdonald *Monchique Resort & Spa (macdonaldmonchique.com)* offers massages.

NIGHTLIFE

FRIDAYHAPPINESS ASSOCIAÇÃO

This is a gloriously eccentric place. Volunteers run this hippyish farm and organise the legendary *Pizzanight Algarve* every Friday. For 20 euros per month, you can become a member of the association (you can also join for just one month, or simply pay

25 euros to support the reforestation needed after the devastating 2021 forest fire) and come and join the party, including the Wednesday jam session and other events. The party goes on into the small hours with music and dancing; it is always full of an interesting mix of people. *Fri from 6pm | Tojeiro, between Marmelete and the Autódromo | fridayhappiness.org*

AROUND MONCHIQUE

❷ MEDRONHO DISTILLERY

2km north of Monchique / around 5 mins by car on the M501

Once you've tried a glass of ✅ medronho you may want to learn more about this fiery regional spirit. In which case, pay a visit to Senhor António *(tel. 2 82 91 27 10)* and his distillery near the hamlet of Mata Porcas. He also makes honey which he puts to excellent use in the significantly sweeter *melosa (medronho + honey + cinnamon)*. You will find both of these in supermarkets, but they're often produced using industrial processes. Senhor António's drinks taste significantly better. 🕮 *F4*

INSIDER TIP

Just a tiny sip ...

❸ FÓIA

8km west of Monchique / 15 mins by car on the N266-3

After the captivating drive from Monchique, you know you have reached the summit when you can see the disconcerting array of aerials and radar units on the 902m-high plateau. Despite this modern eyesore, the view from here is sensational! Throw on a jacket as it can get quite

---

MEDRONHO: STRAWBERRY JUICE FOR GROWN-UPS

⚑ *Medronho* is distilled from the ripe fruits of the strawberry tree (or arbutus) but doesn't actually have anything to do with strawberries aside from its bright colour. In the autumn, local farmers painstakingly harvest the fruit up in the mountains, as the *medronheiro* can't be cultivated in orchards. Around 8kg of fruit are needed to produce just one litre of fiery spirit in the spring.

In other words, it's hard work out in the fields … and in the distillery too, as the *aguardente de medronho* needs to flow evenly out of the still so the temperature needs to be kept constant. This means fires burning day and night, and whole families (often with neighbours) helping out, until the wooden barrels that the fruits have spent the whole winter fermenting in are finally empty and the bottles are full.

Not everybody who distils this brandy at home has a licence to do so, but the authorities will often turn a blind eye in order to preserve the tradition.

windy. Deserted farms and villages and the remnants of painstaking terracing bear silent testimony to a once-thriving agricultural lifestyle.

When driving down, after about 2km stop at the *Miradouro da Fonte Santa* to the right and you'll find a 🌿 spring (*fonte*) where you can get some cool, fresh mountain water. 💷 *F4*

4 PICOTA

4km east of Monchique / around 1 hr on foot

The view from this 773m-high granite peak is perhaps even more stunning than that from Fóia. On a clear day you will be able to see the entire coastline and the magnificent Alentejo region. You can get to the top via a dirt track signposted from the road to Alferce; however, it's much nicer to climb Picota via the well-marked *Via Algarviana* trail (around 6km there and back), which leads through some wonderful cork oak forests (most of which escaped the 2018 forest fires). 💷 *F4*

5 CALDAS DE MONCHIQUE ⭐

5km south of Monchique / 8 mins by car on the N266

These spring waters have been attracting visitors since the Romans started using them to cure rheumatism, skin disorders and respiratory illnesses. Today, the belle époque-style buildings have been restored and new buildings added to create a beautiful small resort. Two million litres of water a day bubble up from the thermal springs; some of it is bottled and sold as *Água de Monchique* throughout Portugal. Those who don't fancy

spending the night here can still enjoy a stroll, taking in the fresh air and romantic atmosphere of the resort. For a stop, the simple but friendly and surprisingly good and inexpensive grilled chicken restaurant *Café Império (closed Tue/Wed | N266 No. 240 | tel. 2 82 91 22 90 | €)* is a good option. It's located a little higher up on the road, but can be reached from the thermal spa complex via a short footpath through the Parque Fonte dos Amores. 💷 *F4*

LOULÉ

(💷 *L6*) **A town that loves to party! Loulé's population makes the most of any opportunity for a celebration. It is one of the most important carnival towns in Portugal and, soon after Easter, the religious festival Mãe Soberana fills the streets with processions and onlookers. In the summer, the annual MED World Music Festival offers a more secular reason to celebrate, with stages placed all around the old town.**

But even without a festival, ⭐ Loulé (pop. 25,000) is a charming small town to visit. It is a place best explored on foot – take some time to stroll through the pretty, narrow streets in the old town, with their relics from the Moorish era, before browsing in some of the delightful shops here. After that, make sure you pay a visit to the *market hall*. With its onion domes and horseshoe arches, this

The Festa da Mãe Soberana is one of many important festivals in Loulé

neo-Moorish building – opened in 1908 – can't fail to catch the eye of all who pass it. Yet it's the interior that will really blow you away: crowds (especially on Saturdays) bustle around enticingly laid-out stalls selling not only fruit, vegetables, bread, cheese and fish, but also a large selection of handicrafts, ceramics and regional products such as cork items. The fact that the market hall is the town's most impressive building is clear from its prominent position directly on Loulé's main street, next door to the old town hall. Behind it, the streets of the old town lead off towards the church or the castle. This is the heart of the former Moorish settlement of Al-Ulyá – "the higher up" – so-called because Loulé is situated on the fertile hills of the Barrocal.

SIGHTSEEING

CASTELO & MUSEU DE LOULÉ

Parts of the 12th-century Moorish castle are now home to Loulé's municipal museum, which is worth visiting for one key reason: you can climb the towers of the castle and view the town from above! It also houses an interesting archaeological exhibition (with Roman amphorae and ceramics), as well as a fully furnished farmer's kitchen from the mid-20th century. *Tue–Sat 10.30am–1.30pm and 2.30–6pm | admission 1.62 euros | Rua D Paio Peres Correia 17 | museudeloule.pt | ⏱ 45 mins*

NOSSA SENHORA DA PIEDADE

The modern pilgrims' church perched on a hill a little to the west of the town

A street in Loulé's old town covered with colourful sun shades

looks a bit like a UFO and makes the neighbouring Renaissance chapel (built in 1553) look rather insubstantial. The latter was much too small to accommodate the annual *Festa da Mãe Soberana* – one of the biggest Marian celebrations in Portugal. For the past 500 years, every Easter Sunday eight strong local men have hauled a 360kg statue of the Virgin Mary down from here to the Franciscan church for the start of this festival. Two weeks later, they have to drag it all the way back as the celebrations reach their peak. For reasons probably best known to them, they do this at break-neck speed.

OLD TOWN

In reality this only consists of two or three streets that lead from the castle to the church, but they are so picturesque that you'll find any excuse to stroll up and down them more than once. At the northern end of the small *centro histórico*, opposite the castle, the ☛ *Nossa Senhora da Conceição (closed Sun/Mon | admission free)* is worth a look – not only for its beautiful *azulejos* and 18th-century gilded wood carving but also for the remains of the Moorish city wall that are displayed underneath the glass floor.

INSIDER TIP
Terrific tiles

A little further along, on the cosy *Largo Dom Pedro I*, archaeologists have been working for years to unearth a Moorish hammam. It is hidden beneath the 15th-century mansion 🐗 *Casa Senhorial dos Barreto (Tue–Sun 10am–12.30pm and 1.30–6pm | admission free | 15-min walk)* You can also find traces of the town's Islamic heritage at the *Igreja de São Clemente* parish church at the southern end of the old town: Christians built this 13th-century church on top of the old mosque (as was so often the case) and used the minaret as the bell tower. Across the way, on the site of what used to be a Moorish cemetery, you can relax under monkey puzzle trees in the *Jardim dos Amuados*.

EATING & DRINKING

11 DA VILLA

The young team at this bistro and tapas bar in the heart of the old town breathes new culinary life into its ancient walls. The world food menu here is constantly changing – they couldn't let people get bored, after all! They're also famous for their regular live music. Don't forget to book, give it a try, and simply enjoy your evening! *Closed Sun lunchtime | Largo D Pedro I. | tel. 9 15 74 49 72 | FB | €€*

BOCAGE

This place looks completely unprepossessing from the outside, and the interior is rather plain too – but the food is truly delicious! Traditional Algarve dishes are served here without any frills, and there are affordable lunch menus too. Reservations are recommended as it gets booked up (understandably!). *Closed Sun | Rua Bocage 14 | tel. 28 90 41 24 16 | restaurantbocage. com | €€*

CAFÉ CALÇINHA

Once illiterate, António Aleixo went on to become a politically engaged but romantic poet, well-known throughout Portugal. His presence, immortalised in bronze, still graces the entrance to his favourite café 75 years after his death. The café itself has been restored but has retained its refined European coffeehouse flair. Alongside coffee and cake, it serves hearty snacks and main courses. The café hosts readings, fado performances and piano concerts some evenings. *Closed Mon | Praça da República | tel. 9 34 25 00 79 | FB | €*

> **INSIDER TIP**
> Coffee, cake and culture

SHOPPING

All great shopping experiences in Loulé revolve around the grand *covered market (Mon–Sat 7am–3pm)*. It's a great place to pick up hand-crafted pieces and culinary delights. On Saturday mornings, there is an additional weekly produce market in the area around the main hall.

Nice little shops and craft boutiques can be found in the pedestrian precinct *Rua 5 de Outubro*, along Praça da República and in the old town.

Take a short break in the churchyard of Barranco do Velho

AROUND LOULÉ

6 ALTE

25km northwest of Loulé / 30 mins by car on the N124

Fig and orange groves surround the village (pop. 1,750). Charming squares, natural springs, a brook, narrow streets and beautiful balcony balustrades decorated with hanging baskets in myriad colours all give Alte a traditional rural atmosphere. The village is also well known for its astonishingly excessive carnival celebrations (but you may not believe this if you visit at other times of the year). ◫ *K5*

7 ROCHA DA PENA

21km north of Loulé / 30 mins by car on the EM525

Incredible cliffs and boulders, 120 species of bird and 500 different plants: the best way to get a sense of this natural paradise is a circular walk. Start at the *Bar das Grutas* at the base of the plateau and start climbing. You need to ascend 200m to reach the top of the plateau at 485m. Head to the northern edge for a stunning view over the Serra do Caldeirão. After that, just walk around – there are superb views in every direction from up here. Head back after exploring the hamlet of Penina (and its small bar). ◫ *K5*

8 SALIR

15km north of Loulé / 20 mins by car on the EM525

Salir (pop. 2,500) is a typical village in the Algarve hinterland. Of the Moorish fort on a hill, all that is visible today are the remnants of a few walls. The area around the hill was occupied as far back as 4,000 years ago. A scenic route on the N124 takes you from the fort (keep a look out for eagles that circle over the cork oak and eucalyptus groves) to *Barranco do Velho*, which is over the regional border in the Serra do Caldeirão. Here, the long-established restaurant *Tia Bia (closed Mon | tel. 2 89 84 64 25 | atiabia.com | €–€€)* offers a gem of Algarvian home cooking at its finest. If you have time, it is far more pleasant to walk this route along Stage 6 of the *Via Algarviana*. If you start in Barranco and head back to Salir, it is even downhill! *(15km, approx. 5 hrs walking).* ⊞ *L5*

INSIDER TIP
Try the migas!

9 FONTE BENÉMOLA

10km north of Loulé / 15 mins by car on the EM525

Fonte Benémola is a stunning, tranquil rural area containing a multitude of natural springs. It is a great place for a picnic or a 4.5km circular trail that will lead you around the area. On the way to the car park at the head of the trail, you will pass *Querença*, a charming village that is worth a stop. Take a stroll to the pretty church square with its village cafés. ⊞ *M5*

10 SÃO BRÁS DE ALPORTEL

13km east of Loulé / 18 mins by car on the N270

This small and quite provincial town (pop. 11,250) has two great indoor attractions – making it ideal for any rainy days. The first is the ❷ *Eco Cork Factory (45-min tour Mon–Fri 11.30am | admission 16.50 euros, book online 24 hrs in advance | Sítio da Mesquita Baixa | eco-corkfactory.com),* where you can discover how tree bark is converted into bottle stops (and a host of other products). It is also well worth paying a visit to the town's small museum, the *Museu do Traje*

(Mon–Fri 10am–1pm and 2–5pm, Sat and Sun 2–5pm | admission 2.50 euros | Rua Dr José Dias Sancho 61 | museu-sbras.com | ⏱ 1 hr). It is the beating cultural heart of the town, and has constantly changing exhibitions, a nice café and a courtyard full of beautiful historic carriages. ⊞ *N6*

SLEEP WELL IN THE HINTERLAND

CLOSE TO THE HEAVENS

Stargaze in a saltwater pool, practise yoga on the sundeck, enjoy the view at 550m, unwind in a hammock shaded by cork oaks: the newly renovated mountain hotel *VilaFoia (12 rooms | Corte Pereiro, Monchique | tel. 2 82 91 01 10 | vila foia.com |€€)* is perfect if you're looking for respite in nature. The hotel isn't far from the highest peak in the Algarve, and you'll definitely need a car to get here.

HISTORIC, BUT NOT DUSTY

The bright *Loulé Jardim Hotel (52 rooms | Praça Manuel de Arriaga | tel. 2 89 41 30 94 | loulejardim hotel.com | €€),* decorated with plenty of plants, has been Loulé's main hotel for many years – but it's still bang up to date. You can get everywhere you need on foot and then relax by the pool on the sun terrace. There is a free car park for your hire car, and the breakfast is top notch!

DISCOVERY TOURS

Want to get under the skin of the region? Then our discovery tours provide the perfect guide – they include advice on which sights to visit, tips on where to stop for that perfect holiday snap, a choice of the best places to eat and drink and suggestions for fun activities.

Cycle to Cacela Velha and enjoy the view of the Ria Formosa

DISCOVERY TOURS OVERVIEW

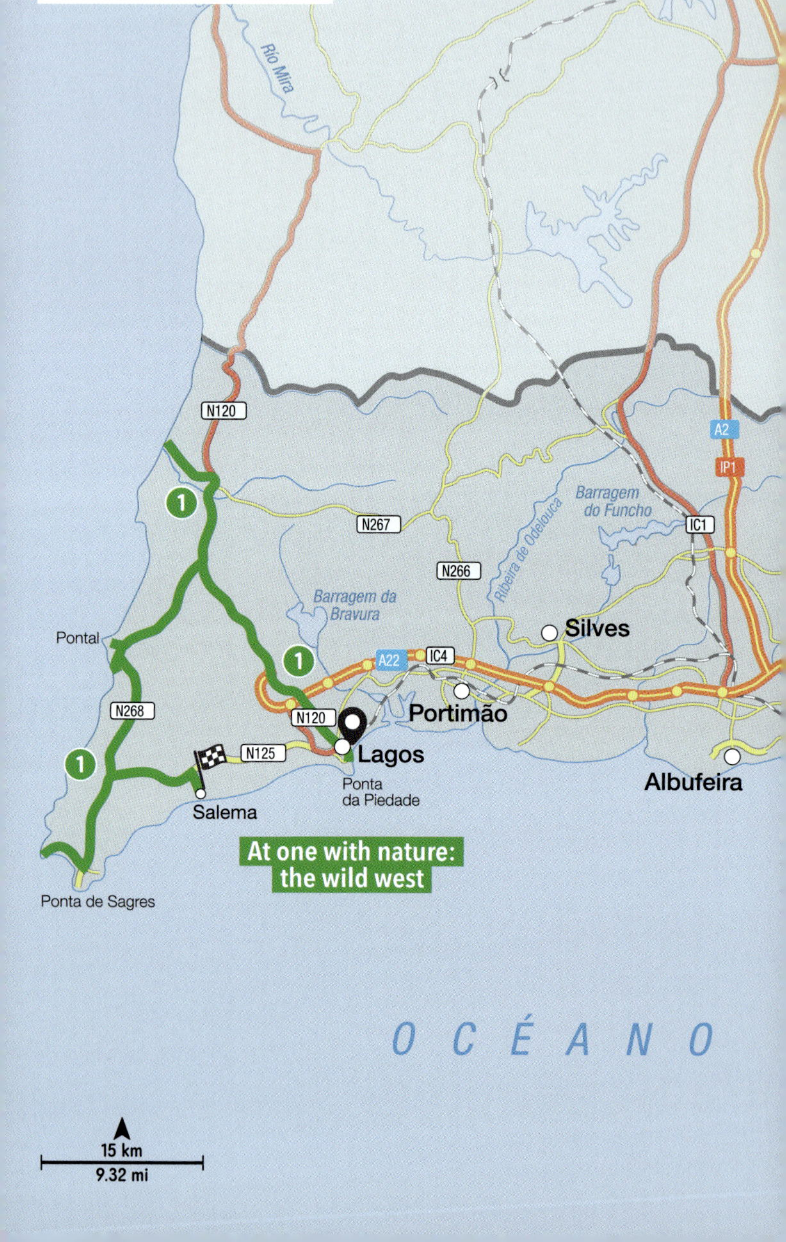

A2
IP1

A2
IP1

Rio Mira

N120

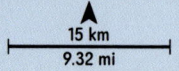

N267

Barragem do Funcho

Ribeira de Odelouca

IC1

N266

Barragem da Bravura

Silves

Pontal

A22   IC4

Portimão

N268

N120

Lagos

N125

Ponta da Piedade

Salema

At one with nature: the wild west

Albufeira

Ponta de Sagres

O C É A N O

15 km
9.32 mi

❶ AT ONE WITH NATURE: THE WILD WEST

➤ Buy biscuits and more in Aljezur's lively covered market
➤ Immerse yourself in largely untouched coastal nature on the Costa Vicentina
➤ Swim at remote beaches
➤ Enjoy spectacular views from Europe's most southwesterly point
➤ Taste the last hotdog this side of the Atlantic
➤ Sip a sundowner in Salema

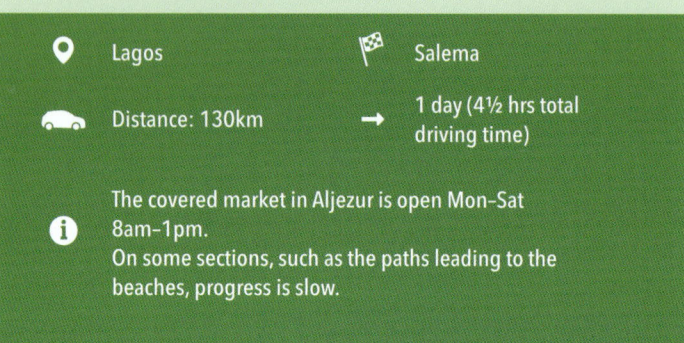

📍 Lagos   🏁 Salema

🚗 Distance: 130km   → 1 day (4½ hrs total driving time)

ℹ️ The covered market in Aljezur is open Mon–Sat 8am–1pm.
On some sections, such as the paths leading to the beaches, progress is slow.

DELICIOUS BISCUITS ON THE WAY TO A RUINED FORT

❶ Lagos
32.5km 32 mins

❷ Aljezur
8.5km 48 mins

From ❶ Lagos ➤ p. 70 *take the N120 northwest towards Bensafrim* and you will soon encounter fertile agricultural land in varying shades of green, occasionally interrupted by dots of orange and yellow from citrus fruit trees – definitely a stark contrast to the Algarve's coast! Pass through Bensafrim, after which the N120 takes you up and down through scrubland and past eucalyptus, pine and cork trees until you meet the main road from Sagres on your left. Your first destination for today is ❷ Aljezur ➤ p. 104. Park up on the patch of gravel beyond the bridge on the right directly opposite the covered market. Make sure to pick up some *Delicias de Aljezur* here, small biscuits which come in three flavours: almond, sweet potato or carob. You are best off exploring the historical part of Aljezur on foot. Start by crossing the bridge and then

INSIDER TIP
Brilliant biccies

head up to the **fortress** through the narrow streets. You get amazing views of the sea from up here. As this name implies, Aljezur was once a Moorish town and this was their lookout.

ONE OF THE MOST BEAUTIFUL BAYS

Now it's time to drive to the Costa Vicentina. *Just a few kilometres northwest of Aljezur*, the ❸ **Praia da Amoreira** (signposted turn-off) stretches out and is admired by both locals and visitors as one of Portugal's most captivating bays on the west coast. Don't miss the chance to dive into the Atlantic here! Splashing around

❸ Praia da Amoreira

7.5km 15 mins

4 Pont'a Pé

21.5km | 14 mins

in the water will have woken your appetite in you, so after this short detour to the beach, jump back in the car and head on to **4 Pont'a Pé ➤ p. 106**, a nearby trendy restaurant. Almost every dish on the menu is served with local sweet potatoes.

A LAGOON AND A STROLL WITH A VIEW

After your meal, *take the N268 heading south from Aljezur* through a sparsely populated region. You will reach Bordeira on your left but carry on to the next town of Carrapateira ➤ p. 108. *Take a right down to* **5 Praia da Bordeira**, where sand dunes separate a lagoon from the sea. Take advantage of the proximity to one of the Algarve's best long-distance paths and take a stroll on the *Rota Vicentina*. From the path, you will get great views of the beach below. You can theoretically carry on to the next beach (about 7km). Quite a lot of people also drive on this dirt track, but save the walkers a cloud of dust and *hit the proper road again before heading to the* **6 Praia do Amado**, a beach much loved by surfers.

5 Praia da Bordeira

4km | 9 mins

6 Praia do Amado

30km | 35 mins

A LIGHTHOUSE AND FRESH FISH

Back on the main road, drive through Vila do Bispo and the port town of Sagres ➤ p. 100 to **7 Cabo de São**

7 Cabo de São Vicente

Tourist honeypot: Cabo de São Vicente

Vicente ➤ p. 103. The rugged coastal panorama around the lighthouse is unrivalled. If you are hungry here, pick up a sausage from the German hot dog stand. Finish your tour by *driving off the N125 for a last detour to Portugal's southern coast.* Your destination is ❽ **Salema** with its splendid beach. Slowly unwind by taking a dip in the Atlantic or a bite to eat in one of the town's bars and restaurants such as **A Boia** ➤ **p. 78**, which offers a special location and serves great seafood.

24km 24 mins

❽ Salema

❷ HISTORY & CULTURE ON THE BORDER: THE UNDISCOVERED EAST

- ➤ **Absorb the view from Castro Marim's castle**
- ➤ **Birdwatch in the wetlands by the border**
- ➤ **Gasp at the panoramic views along the Rio Guadiana**
- ➤ **Take a zipline across the river in Alcoutim**
- ➤ **Make a detour to Alentejo and travel back to the Moorish period**
- ➤ **Enjoy sun, swimming and delicious food in Vila Real de Santo António**

📍 Castro Marim 🏁 Vila Real de Santo António

🚗 Distance: 160km ➡ 1 day (3½ hrs total driving time)

ⓘ Don't forget your binoculars!
Note that tourist sites in Mértola are closed on Mondays. Reserve a zipline at *tel. 0034 670 313 933* in Spain or *limitezero.com*

TIME TRAVEL IN THE CASTELO

Let the time travel commence! Start this tour with a visit to ❶ **Castro Marim** ➤ **p. 63**, 6km to the north of Vila Real. You will spot the **castelo** perching on a hill from some distance away. It is well worth a visit and takes you high up to the town. The castle, which was home to the

❶ Castro Marim

37.5km 50 mins

The Islamic interior has been conserved in Mértola's Igreja Matriz

influential Military Order of Christ back in the 14th century, is crying out for you to conquer it! It's a long (sweaty) slog up, but you will be rewarded with stunning views over the Rio Guadiana lowlands and the Reserva Natural do Sapal de Castro Marim ➤ p. 64 where you may be able to see the flamingos frolicking.

SOME LEISURELY TWITCHING BEFORE A HIGH-OCTANE BORDER CROSSING

After visiting the castle, *head north on the N122 (IC27). Approximately 12km after Castro Marim, turn right to Foz de Odeleite taking the riverside road along the wide and tidal* Rio Guadiana ➤ p. 61. The views from this road are incredible! The river, which marks the border with Spain, is 744km long yet only the last 50km stretch before its estuary is navigable. The neighbouring valleys are home to many bird species, some of which are rare and endangered.

❷ Alcoutim

45.5km 1 hr

Take a longer break in ❷ Alcoutim ➤ p. 65 where you can experience perhaps the most James Bond border

crossing in Europe! ✅ Instead of check-points and traffic jams, here you can fly across from Spain on a zipline! **Limitezero** *(daily summer 10am–2pm and 4–8pm, otherwise Wed–Sun 10.30am–2pm and 3.30–7pm. They are based in Spain, so all times are in Spanish time – one hour later than Portugal)* are the people who can make this happen for you. The zipline is over 700m long and reaches maximum speeds of 80kmh. The line starts in Sanlúcar de Guadiana on the Spanish side – which you can reach by a frequent ferry – and the journey lasts approximately three minutes. Anyone who thinks the zipline may be too high octane can spend some (sedate) time visiting the secluded **castelo** in Alcoutim. There are a few decent lunch spots near the shore, but the tapas bar and café **Beira Rio** *(closed Wed | €)* is one of the best.

HISTORY THAT WILL HAVE YOU COMING BACK FOR MOOR

After lunch, get back in the car and drive through a virtually uninhabited region before reaching the Alentejo. The castle of ❸ **Mértola** suddenly appears in front of you. Narrow streets wind between small whitewashed houses up to the parish church of **Igreja Matriz**. There is nowhere else in the region where the presence of Islamic Portugal can be so keenly felt as here with its hoof-shaped entrance and Islamic *mihrab* (prayer niche) facing Mecca. This is because the Christians simply continued to use the old mosque after the Reconquista – unique in Portugal. The town's highlight is the castle with its impos-ing tower, the **Torre de Menagem**. Enjoy the view and then a refreshment in one of the cafés in the lower part of town.

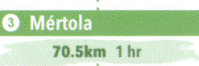

❸ **Mértola**

70.5km 1 hr

RESERVOIR, BEACH AND TOWN

Head *south from Mértola on the N122 (IC27)* directly back to Vila Real de Santo António without any more major detours. On the last section of this route, you'll notice on your right the reservoir (Barragem) of Odeleite. Before finishing your day in town, first *drive along a partly bumpy road for a few kilometres following the river until you reach a turn-off to the right*, at the end of which is the car park for the ④ **Praia de Santo António** – a vast stretch of beach unknown to many tourists, which extends almost to the mouth of the Rio Guadiana and is surrounded by sand dunes. After a spot of (sun) bathing, take a leisurely stroll around the historical centre of ⑤ **Vila Real de Santo António ➤ p. 61** before the pangs of hunger start to get too strong. There are lots of good places to sate them on the main square, but one that it is popular with locals and tourists alike is **Puro Café** *(daily | Rua 5 de Outubro 13 | tel. 2 81 51 24 99 | €)*.

④ Praia de Santo António

4.5km 10 mins

⑤ Vila Real de Santo António

③ THROUGH THE UNSPOILT HINTERLAND

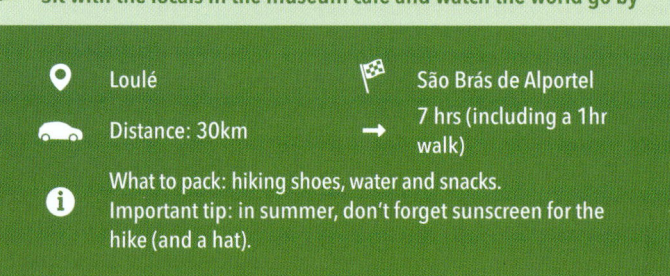

➤ Food shop in the Algarve's most beautiful covered market
➤ Enjoy time-honoured coffee-house culture in Loulé
➤ Take a circular walk to a refreshing natural spring
➤ Experience cork and culture in the sleepy town of São Brás de Alportel
➤ Sit with the locals in the museum café and watch the world go by

📍 Loulé   🏁 São Brás de Alportel

🚗 Distance: 30km   → 7 hrs (including a 1hr walk)

ⓘ What to pack: hiking shoes, water and snacks.
Important tip: in summer, don't forget sunscreen for the hike (and a hat).

SENSORY STIMULATION TO START TO THE DAY

Start in ① **Loulé ➤ p. 122**. Let yourself get lost among the fresh bread, flowers, figs and fish at the **market** and stock up on supplies for your hike later. You will still

① Loulé

14.5km   45 mins

Loulé market is a riot of colour and a feast for the senses

have some time left over for a stroll through the town to visit the **castelo**. If this puts you in the mood for a second breakfast, **Café Calcinha** *(Praça da República | FB | €)* is an ideal place to chill out before getting in the car.

WALK THROUGH LUSH COUNTRYSIDE

Suitably replete, jump in the car and *set off in a northeasterly direction to Querença, where you then follow the signs* to the small 392-hectare natural reserve of **❷ Fonte Benémola**. The circular walking route is

❷ Fonte Benémola

17.5km 1 hr

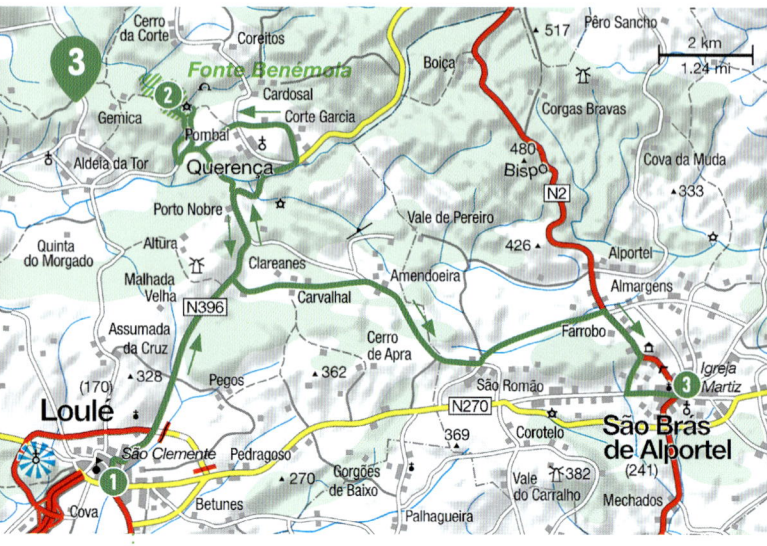

signposted with yellow and red markings, is about 4.5km in total, and should not be too strenuous. You will be grateful (especially in summer) that *you mostly walk along a lush green valley*. Once you reach the babbling Benémola spring, it will be time to stop and tuck into your picnic in the shade of the many trees here. After a decent rest (don't forget to fill your water bottles), *simply cross the crystal-clear water using the concrete bollards and head back to your car on the other side of the river.*

CULTURAL IMMERSION

Continue on the N396 and the N2 until you reach the old cork town of ❸ São Brás de Alportel ➤ p. 127, where cork products are still made today. You'll arrive in the afternoon when the Museu do Traje ➤ p. 127 is open. This is not your typical, dusty local museum specialising in traditional folk dress, but rather a cultural centre which regularly hosts interesting events. A fascinating side wing is dedicated to explaining the extraction and production of cork and its courtyard houses a collection of historic carriages. The museum's bar with its delightful summer terrace is the perfect way to end your day trip.

❸ São Brás de Alportel

④ CYCLE FROM TAVIRA TO VILA REAL DE SANTO ANTÓNIO

➤ Cycle along beautiful coastal paths
➤ Pedal across salt marshes and through coastal forests
➤ Take in great views of the Ria Formosa in Cacela Velha
➤ Stop for refreshments and a beach break in Manta Rota
➤ Detour to the Sapal de Castro Marim bird sanctuary
➤ Visit a salt producer

📍 Tavira

🏁 Vila Real de Santo António

→ 45km

🚲 1 day (approx. 3½hrs total cycling time)

ℹ️ You can rent a bike, e.g. in Tavira through *Abilio (abilio-bikes.com)*.
It can get very hot at the height of summer as there's hardly any shade en route.
You can take the train from VRSA back to the starting point in Tavira *(departures roughly hourly | 25 mins | 2.95 euros | cp.pt)*. Bike transport is free, but you will be turned away if the train is full.

FROM TAVIRA TO CACELA VELHA

The *Ecovia Litoral* runs for over 214km along the entire Algarve coast, from the Spanish border to Cabo de São Vicente; sometimes you'll be cycling along lovely cycle tracks and sometimes along busy thoroughfares. The route described here is pleasant to cycle and largely well signposted with yellow and blue markers.

By the Rio Gilão in ❶  *Tavira* ➤ p. 55 *get on your bike and head east towards the Plaza shopping centre. Turn off here into the* ❷ *Ria Formosa Natural Park; soon,* the wetlands and salt flats of this nature reserve will come into view. You can *get to Conceição via gravel paths and a wooden bridge; you will then pass several orange plantations and a golf course before reaching the picturesque village of* ❸  *Cacela Velha* ➤ p. 61.

❶ Tavira
3.5km 15 mins
❷ Ria Formosa Natural park
9.5km 50 mins
❸ Cacela Velha

Keep your eyes peeled in the Rio Formosa reserve, and you might spot a greenshank!

3km 10 mins

Enjoy the view over the easternmost lagoon of the Ria Formosa from the old coastal fortress.

BEACH BREAK IN MANTA ROTA

❹ Manta Rota

Further along the route, at ❹ Manta Rota, take a little break by detouring to the Praia da Lota, where you can dive into the Atlantic and then fortify yourself with fresh fish at the local beach restaurant Dona Lota *(daily in summer, closed in winter | tel. 9 61 33 75 09 | €€).* To continue on your journey, from *behind the neighbouring village of Altura, the route will take you briefly along the N125 (watch out for traffic) before turning off southwards at the sign for "Cabeço".*

THROUGH BEAUTIFUL COASTAL FORESTS

10km 50 mins

Behind the neighbourhood of Retur, there is a particularly lovely part of the route that starts in the car park of the Praia de Adão e Eva *and takes you along sandy paths shaded by tall trees. After 1km, you will reach the*

❺ Monte Gordo

holiday resort of ❺ Monte Gordo ➤ p. 62. Treat yourself to a home-made Italian ice cream at Geladaria Baunilha & Chocolate *(closed Mon | Av. Infante D Henrique 8)* on the waterside promenade. *On the route to Vila Real de Santo António, the M511 runs through a pine forest that has been classified as a Mata Nacional (national forest).*

INTO CASTRO MARIM NATURE RESERVE

Prefer nature to the big city? *At the first roundabout in Vila Real, head north. The N122, which has a cycle lane, will take you straight to* ❻ **Sapal de Castro Marim bird reserve** ➤ p. 64. Here, you can watch the birds, enjoy the magnificent wetland scenery, and take a selfie with the bronze (naked!) cyclist. *Just after the hiker statue, which you will see after 1km, you can visit salt producer* ❼ **Jorge Raiado** (Salmarim | *usually open afternoons, otherwise upon request* | *tel. 9 66 92 24 37* | *salmarim. com), at the entrance to Castro Marim, surrounded by salt marshes, where you can buy a special flor-de-sal pot as a souvenir. Then whizz back to* ❽ **Vila Real de Santo António** ➤ p. 61. *Immediately after crossing the railway line, turn left towards the railway station*, which was built in 1945 in a beautiful modernist style.

12km 45 mins

❻ **Sapal de Castro Marim bird reserve**

5km 20 mins

❼ **Jorge Raiado**

2km 8 mins

❽ **Vila Real de Santo António**

3 km
1.86 mi

GOOD TO KNOW

HOLIDAY BASICS

ARRIVAL

GETTING THERE

It is possible to drive or take the train from the UK to the Algarve if you have the time and the stamina – both of these options will take up to two days. Less green, but cheaper and easier, is to take advantage of the huge number of flights from various UK airports to Faro. Depending on the point of departure, the flight takes about 2½ hours and is offered by virtually every major airline. Prices vary and booking early is advisable, especially if you intend to go in the summer.

All the information you could possibly need about Faro airport is online at *ana.pt.* On arrival, once you have got through all the formalities, you will find a large range of car hire companies in the Arrivals hall. There are also always lots of taxis in the rank just outside the terminal building. To get to the centre of the city, you have two options: take a taxi, which should cost around 15 euros and can be pre-booked on the (unofficial) website: *aeroportodefaro.com/taxis*. Or you can take a no. 14 or no. 16 bus (2.70 euros), although the buses only depart at irregular intervals, mostly just once an hour. The bus stop is by the short-stay car park, opposite the taxi rank – the one with the *Próximo (proximo.pt)* timetable. Both buses go to the central bus station in the city

Portugal uses GMT (and clocks change on the same dates as in the UK), so it is always the same time in the Algarve as in the UK and Ireland.

centre, from where you can easily change buses to reach every corner of the Algarve.

If you want to combine a trip to the Algarve with a city break in Lisbon, you can fly directly to Lisbon, spend a couple of days in the capital and then take a bus or train to the south. The train from Lisbon to Lagos (change at Tunes) takes about four hours and should cost from 24.15 euros, if booked in advance; Lisbon to Faro costs from 23.55 euros. There are also long-distance bus options, (e.g. *flix bus.pt* or *re-de-expressos.pt*) from Lisbon's main bus stations to all the major destinations in the Algarve, taking about three hours and costing from 5 euros.

GETTING IN

UK and other non-EU citizens do not need to apply for a visa for visits of up to 90 days. For longer trips, check the

OFFSET YOUR FLIGHT

The return flight is likely to be the most environmentally damaging part of your holiday. A single traveller on a return flight from London to Faro generates 584kg of CO_2. You can offset this emission at *co2.myclimate.org/en/flight_ calculators/new* (and other organisations) for around £17. The money is used to fund climate protection projects around the world.

Portuguese embassy homepage. EU citizens can travel freely to Portugal with no restrictions on length of stay.

CLIMATE & WHEN TO GO

Europe's most southwesterly region lies on the Atlantic Ocean but has a mild Mediterranean climate and does not get snow in the winter. During the summer months between May and October it can get particularly hot. Check the chart (p. 150) to get an idea of the weather when you are going, but generally it is wise to pack a jumper or jacket for cooler evenings. It practically never rains in summer, although showers may occur during transition periods between the seasons, so it's worth packing a light raincoat.

GETTING AROUND

CAR HIRE & DRIVING
For the best prices, book in advance (from 80 euros/week for a small car). You have to be 21 years of age to hire a car or motorbike, and you'll usually need your passport, driving licence and a credit card. All major car hire companies have branches at Faro airport; some will bring your car directly to your accommodation for an additional charge. If you want to drive on the A2 motorway, you will need to pay the tolls at toll stations. Speed limits for cars are 50kph in urban areas, 90kph on open roads and 120kph on motorways. EU blood alcohol limits apply: 0.5g of alcohol per litre of blood (or 0.2g for some drivers).

PUBLIC TRANSPORT 🍃
All the bigger destinations in the Algarve are well served by buses, both within individual towns and between them. You can travel by bus from the Algarve to Lisbon in about three hours; it's not expensive. For timetables and tickets, check the website of the company that operates on the route you want to take (eva-bus.com, frotazul-algarve.pt, rede-expressos.pt).

The Algarve coast between Lagos and Vila Real de Santo António is well served by trains too (cp.pt). Some stretches, such as the one that runs from Faro to Tavira past the lagunas of the Ria Formosa, are stunningly beautiful. The stations in Faro, Tavira, Portimão and Lagos are in the middle of town; the station for Albufeira is Ferreiras, which is 5km from town.

INSIDER TIP
Take the train

TAXI
The taxi metre will show the exact fare. There are surcharges for suitcases and late-night/weekend trips. Alternative ride services, such as Uber and Bolt, which you can use via their apps, are cheaper than official taxis

EMERGENCIES

CONSULATES & EMBASSIES
British Vice Consulate in Portimão
Edificio A Fábrica, Av. Guanaré, 8501-915 Portimao | gov.uk/world/organisa tions/british-vice-consulate-portimao

United States Embassy in Lisbon
Av. das Forças Armadas, Sete-Rios, 1600-081 Lisbon | tel. 2 17 27 33 00 | pt.usembassy.gov

EMERGENCY SERVICES

Call 112 for police, fire brigade and ambulance.

HEALTH

Make sure your travel insurance includes comprehensive health insurance. It should cover treatment in the accident and emergency department *(urgências)* of local GP clinics *(centros de saúde)* or state-run hospitals *(hospital)*. Some policies will allow you to be treated by a private hospital or a doctors' practice where waiting times will be shorter and where English is also often spoken. You may, however, have to pay your bill upfront so it is imperative that you keep all treatment and medication invoices.

Pharmacies *(farmácias)* are useful for any prescription-only medication but, as in the UK, lots of basic medication can be procured off the shelf in supermarkets.

ESSENTIALS

ACCOMMODATION

There is an extraordinary range of accommodation options in the Algarve, from campsites to the poshest luxury hotels, with plenty of youth hostels *(pousadasjuventude.pt)* and B&Bs in between.

The highest hotel concentration is in the Barlavento, especially in the areas around Albufeira, Armação de Pêra and Portimão (where it could be argued that a beautiful stretch of coast has been ruined). Carvoeiro and Lagos have not been swallowed up to the same extent, while Sagres and its surrounding area is well served by smaller places.

The hotels around Vilamoura and in the "Golden Triangle" around Quinta do Lago are often fairly smart. Faro, Olhão and Tavira have plenty of good places to stay without being overrun. Monte Gordo is the place in the Sotavento most subsumed by mass tourism.

The hinterland and the west coast have very few large hotels. Here you will find a number of lovely smaller places and holiday lets.

BEACHES

The Atlantic is not the Mediterranean and can be subject to dangerous currents and undertows, so the safety flags on beaches really are worth taking into consideration. Blue flags don't tell you anything about the conditions – they mean that the beach itself is particularly clean. It is also worth being aware of signs warning about falling rocks or unstable cliffs. Every year there are fatal accidents on the Algarve caused by its rocky coastline. Those used to the UK/Irish coast will not be surprised by the tidal difference on the Algarve, which can be several metres at different times of day *(tide tables at hidrografico.pt)*.

Topless sunbathing is widely accepted but nudism is only allowed on a small number of beaches – Adegas near Odeceixe, Deserta near Faro and Barril near Tavira.

CAMPING

You will find campsites all over the Algarve – very often in excellent locations (just outside village centres or at the beach). You will see a lot of campervans from all over Europe in the Algarve. For information on where they can be accommodated and for the best campsites, refer to *camping.info/portugal/algarve* and *autocaravan algarve.com*. Wild camping is illegal in Portugal, as is parking up a campervan in a non-official car park. Some places (mainly Sagres and Aljezur) are enforcing these rules with ever greater rigour. Use the websites above to avoid being moved on and/or fined.

CUSTOMS

Visitors from the UK and other countries outside the EU customs union are subject to limits on the import and export of goods as follows: 200 cigarettes or 250g tobacco, 4 litres of spirits (over 22% vol.), 9 litres of spirits (under 22% vol.) or 18 litres of still wine. If you are at all worried about what you are bringing in, check online for up-to-date limits.

DRINKING WATER

Tap water on the coast can taste of chlorine but is safe. In the hinterland, it is beautifully clear and tastes great. You can, of course, buy bottled water in supermarkets if you are at all worried.

INFORMATION

The websites of the national and regional tourist associations, *visit portugal.com* and *visitalgarve.com*, provide all kinds of useful information.

The Algarve's cities and bigger towns all have their own centrally located tourist information office *(posto de turismo)*, where you can get city maps, hiking brochures and more.

LANGUAGE

Unsurprisingly, Portuguese is the language spoken in the Algarve, but you will get by with English in virtually all contexts on the coast. (It is not worth practising your school Spanish; even though it is often understood in Portugal, people can be insulted by its use). In some places in the hinterland, you will have to resort to gestures!

MARKETS

Every town has a regional market or *mercado municipal* where fresh fruit, vegetables, meat and fish can be bought. Generally open Monday to Saturday 8am–1pm, the best of these are in Loulé and Olhão. Aside from these, all the districts *(concelhos)* hold a flea market once a month.

MONEY

The euro is Portugal's currency. There are ATMs everywhere *(multibanco)*. Be aware that your banks may charge fees and that many Portuguese banks will limit you to a maximum of two 200-euro withdrawals a day. Virtually everywhere takes credit cards but having a little cash for the exceptions is a good policy, especially in more remote places.

OPENING HOURS

Many restaurants tend to be closed on either Sunday or Monday in the winter months. In summer it's common for restaurants to be open all week. As a rule, shops are open Monday to Friday 10am–1pm and 3–7pm, Saturday until 1pm. Big supermarkets are open seven days a week, mostly 9am–10pm. Museums and places of interest are often closed on a Monday and/or Sunday. Some museums and other institutions change their opening hours up to five times a year so check online before planning a visit.

POST

Post offices *(CTT* or *correios)* are red and are open Monday to Friday 9am–6pm. Bigger post offices are also open on Saturday morning. There are vending machines for stamps outside most post offices. Postage info: *ctt.pt.*

There's plenty of choice at the markets

PRICES

The cheapest places to do food shopping on the Algarve are international budget supermarket chains. Museum entrance fees start at 2 euros, with reductions for children, students and pensioners. When it comes to food, there's a huge range: you can occasionally get set meals in simple local restaurants for as little as 10 euros, but there are also top chef tastings for over 100 euros.

PUBLIC HOLIDAYS

Local holidays honouring the patron saints take place in many towns and villages. The following are all holidays in the Algarve:

HOW MUCH DOES IT COST?	
Coffee	0.80 euros *for an espresso*
Snack	3.50 euros *for a* bifana *roll*
Wine	3 euros *for a glass of wine in a bar*
Souvenir	6 euros *for a handpainted* azulejo *tile*
Public transport	1.60 euros *for a 10km train journey*
Bicycle	25 euros *for 1-day mountain-bike hire*

1 Jan	Ano Novo (New Year)
Feb/March	Shrove Tuesday
March/April	Good Friday
25 April	Dia de Liberdade (Anniversary of the 1974 Revolution)
1 May	Dia do Trabalhador (Labour Day)
1 June	Corpus Christi
10 June	Dia de Portugal (Portugal Day on the day of death of national poet Luís de Camões)
15 Aug	Assumption
5 Oct	Implantação da República (founding of the Republic 1910)
1 Nov	All Saints' Day
1 Dec	Restauração da Independência (end of the union with Spain 1640)
8 Dec	Imaculada Conceição (Immaculate Conception)
25 Dec	Natal (Christmas)

TELEPHONE & INTERNET

The dialling code for Portugal is +351. Mobile numbers begin with a "9" and landlines with a "2". WiFi is available in all hotels and most cafés and restaurants.

TOILETS

Lots of beach bar toilets (and some in older buildings) are unable to process paper. Use the bins provided.

WEATHER

High season
Low season

	JAN	FEB	MARCH	APRIL	MAY	JUNE	JULY	AUG	SEPT	OCT	NOV	DEC
Daytime temperatures (°C)	15°	16°	18°	20°	22°	25°	28°	28°	26°	22°	19°	16°
Night-time temperatures (°C)	9°	10°	11°	13°	14°	18°	20°	20°	19°	16°	13°	10°
Sunshine hours/day	6	7	7	9	10	12	12	12	10	8	6	6
Rainy days/month	7	6	8	5	3	1	0	0	2	4	7	7
Sea temperatures in °C	15°	15°	15°	16°	17°	18°	19°	20°	20°	19°	17°	16°

☀ Sunshine hours/day   🌂 Rainy days/month   ≋ Sea temperatures in °C

USEFUL PHRASES

SMALLTALK

Yes/no/maybe	sim/não/talvez	seeng/nowng/tal'vesh
Please	se faz favor	se fash fa'vor
Thank you	obrigado (m)/obrigada (f)	obri'gadoo/obri'gada
Good morning/Hello/ Good afternoon/ Goodnight	Bom dia!/Bom dia!/Boa tarde!/Boa noite!	bong 'dia/bong 'dia/'boa 'tard/'boa 'noyt
Hi! Bye!	Olá!/Adeus!	o'la/a'dy-oosh
My name is	Chamo-me ...	'shamoo-me
What is your name? (informal/formal)?	Como te chamas?/Como se chama?	'komoo te 'shamas/ 'komoo se 'shama
I am from	Sou de ...	so döe
Excuse me (informal/ formal)	Desculpa!/Desculpe!	dish'kulpa/dish'kulp
Could you repeat?	Como?	'komoo
I (don't) like this	(Não) gosto disto	(nau) 'goshtoo 'dishtoo
Good/bad	bem/mal	beng/mal
How much ...?	Quanto custa ...?	'kwantoo 'kooshta
Help!/Watch out!	Socorro!/Atenção!	soo'korroo/atten'sowng
Broken/not working	estragado/não funciona	ishtra'gadoo/nowng fung'siona
0/1/2/3/4/5/6/7/8/9/ 10/100/1000	zero/um, uma/dois, duas/ três/quatro/cinco/seis/ sete/oito/nove/dez/ cem/mil	'zeroo/'oong, 'ooma/'doysh, 'dooash/tresh/'kwatroo/ 'seengk'oo/'seysh/'set/' oytoo/'nov/'desh/'seng/meel

EATING & DRINKING

The menu, please	A ementa, se faz favor	a i'menta, se fash fa'vor
Bottle/glass	garrafa/copo	gar'raffa/'koppoo
Salt/pepper/sugar	sal/pimenta/açúcar	sall/pi'menta/a'ssookar
Vinegar/oil	vinagre/azeite	vi'nagre/a'zeite
Knife/fork/spoon	faca/garfo/colher	'faka/'garfoo/kool'yer
Milk/cream/lemon	leite/nata/limão	'läite/'nahta/li'mau
With/without ice/gas	com/sem gelo/gás	kong/seng 'zheloo/gash
Vegetarian	vegetariano/a	vezhhetari'anoo, -a
Allergy	alergia	aller'zhia
The bill, please	A conta, se faz favor	a 'konta, se fash fa'vor
Cash/credit card	em dinheiro/com cartão de crédito	end din'yeyroo/kong kar'twong de 'kreditoo

HOLIDAY VIBES
FOR RELAXATION & CHILLING

FOR BOOKWORMS & FILMBUFFS

300 DAYS OF SUN

If the title alone isn't enough to sell you a book set in the Algarve, Deborah Lawreson's 2016 tightly plotted novel set in Faro tells the story of two different American visitors to the region across 70 years of history.

PEREIRA MAINTAINS

There are not many English-language books set in the Algarve, but to get a fascinating insight into Portugal's history under fascism, you can do a lot worse than Antonio Tabucchi's 1994 masterpiece about a journalist struggling to work in a dictatorship.

ALGARVE THE MOVIE

Turn up the volume and hit play! A surfer movie about the best surf spots and most remote beaches in the western Algarve. There is no dialogue – the images and background music speak for themselves. (Westcoastcampers, 2014, YouTube)

ONE FOOT IN THE ALGARVE

One Foot in the Grave may be a tad dated, but Victor Meldrew's disastrous trip to the Algarve will have even the hippest, most up-to-date holiday-makers literally lol-ing over a glass of Algarve wine. (DVD/Streaming, 1993)

❚❚ SALVADOR SOBRAL – AMAR PELOS DOIS
The soulful winner of Eurovision loves for two in this jazz lament.

▶ NANOOK – MAIS PERTO, SÓ
An Algarve native with a croaky voice, harmonica and guitar. This Faro songster enchants everyone who gives him a listen.

▶ TIAGO BETTENCOURT – CARTA
A song to give you goose bumps by one of the country's most talented musicians.

▶ ANA MOURA – DESFADO
A bit of fado has to be in this list! Even if this one is probably a touch too cheerful …

▶ ANTONIO VARIAÇÕES – CANÇÃO DO ENGATE
One of many superb songs from this talented singer who died when he was only 39.

Your holiday soundtrack can be found on Spotify under MARCO POLO Portugal

Or scan this code with the Spotify app

ONLINE

JOHNNY AFRICA
Johnny Africa's blog entry on the Algarve provides excellent ideas for a trip as well as a whole load of tantalising photos. *(johnnyafrica.com/algarve-portugal-itinerary)*

THE PORTUGALIST
A great guide to the region which also has lots of tips on moving to Portugal should you find yourself wanting more after your holiday. *(portugalist.com/the-algarve)*

ALGARVE BLOG
A blog by two expats with a distinctively artistic slant. Probably no great surprise given that Alyson is a painter and Dave a photographer. Their dog, Kat, plays a pretty major role. *(alyson sheldrake.com/blog)*

O COZINHEIRO ESTE ALGARVE
A blog by a Scottish amateur cook who also runs a guest house near Tavira. Following this blog is one of the easiest ways to learn how to cook authentic Algarve food at home. *(casarosada-algarve.blogspot.com)*

INDEX

154

WE WANT TO HEAR FROM YOU!

Did you have a great holiday? Is there something on your mind? Whatever it is, let us know! Whether you want to praise the guide, alert us to errors or give us a personal tip – MARCO POLO would be pleased to hear from you.
Please contact us by email:

sales@heartwoodpublishing.co.uk

We do everything we can to provide the very latest information for your trip. Nevertheless, despite all of our authors' thorough research, errors can creep in. MARCO POLO does not accept any liability for this.

Credits
Cover Photo: Clifs in the Barlavento region (Shutterstock: trabantos)
Photos: DUMONT Bildarchiv: S. Lubenow (26/27, 33, 52, 63, 86, 123, 149); HUBER-IMAGES: L. Da Ros (91), O. Fantuz (66/67), G. Gräfenhain (104/105), M. Howard (16/17, 73, 84/85, 94), J. Huber (12), S. Kremer (74/75), S. Lubenow (34/35, 60, 71, 78, 101); HUBER-IMAGES/4 Corners: M. Howard (77); laif: F. Heuer (58), C. Zahn (29, 36, 126); laif/hemis.fr: F. Guiziou (96/97); S. Lier (155); lookphotos: T. Roetting (82), T. Stankiewicz (107, 134), B. v. Dierendonck (120); mauritius images: F. Guiziou (40/41), R. Harding (8/9), M. Howard (14/15, 114, 116, 119); mauritius images/AkremaFotoArt (inside flap, outside flap, 1); mauritius images/Alamy: amnat99 (46, 124), Bildagentur-online/McPhoto-Boyungs (49), I. Canham (108), Cro Magnon (2/3, 50/51, 102), J.P. Fernandes (136), N. Ferrin (80/81), A. Gardiner (22), E. Lattes (110/111), H. Weges (21), T. E. White (35); mauritius images/Alamy/Universal Images Group North America LLC: DeAgostini (25); mauritius images/Hemis.fr: R. Mattes (6/7); mauritius images/imageBROKER: D. Rüther (142), G & M Therin-Weise (11); mauritius images/Travel Collection: G. Lengler (139); mauritius images/Warburton-Lee: S. Lubenow (rear flap); picture-alliance/Zoonar: I. Tykhyi (37); Shutterstock: RudiErnst (6/7), Lucian Coman (28/29), DeltaOFF (92/93), f8 studio (128/129), Marcin Krzyzak (152/153), Lux Blue (64), Sopotnicki (54, 88/89, 144/145), SteveWoods (13), Tupungato (32/33), Waclav Sonnek (10)

GPSR Compliance: MairDumont GmbH, Marco-Polo-Str, 73760 Ostfildern, Deutschland. Email: info@marcopolo.de

5th Edition – fully revised and updated 2026
Worldwide Distribution: Heartwood Publishing Ltd, Bath, United Kingdom
www.heartwoodpublishing.co.uk

© MAIRDUMONT GmbH & Co. KG, Ostfildern
Authors: Sara Lier, Rolf Osang
Editor: Petra Klose
Picture editor: Barbara Mehrl
Cartography: © KOMPASS-Karten GmbH, A-6020 Innsbruck/MAIRDUMONT, D-73760 Ostfildern (pp. 38–39, 130–131, 133, 137, 140, 143, outer flap, pull-out map); © KOMPASS-Karten GmbH, kompass.de under licence from © OpenStreetMap Contributors, osm.org/copyright (pp. 42–43, 44, 56, 68–69, 70, 79, 98–99, 112–113)
Cover design and pull-out map cover design: Eggers+Diaper, Aachen
Page design: Langenstein Communication GmbH, Ludwigsburg

Heartwood Publishing credits:
Translated from the German by Rachel Farmer, John Owen, Kathleen Becker, Jennifer Walcoff Neuheiser, Suzanne Kirkbright
Editors: Felicity Laughton, Kate Michell, Sophie Blacksell Jones
Prepress: Summerlane Books, Bath
Printed in India

MARCO POLO AUTHOR
SARA LIER

Sara Lier has been leading tour groups around the Algarve for over 15 years. From the coast to the mountains, from the hinterland to the narrow streets of the towns, she has guided visitors everywhere across the region. Sara loves southern Portugal, where she now lives, both in the quiet winter months and when it is busy in summer!

DOS & DON'TS

HOW TO AVOID SLIP-UPS & BLUNDERS

DON'T WASTE WATER
The Algarve suffers from drought and water scarcity. If things carry on as they are, it will be difficult to keep the landscape green and the pools filled. So make sure you save water when you can.

DON'T PLAY WITH FIRE
You can't be too careful in the dry summer months. Forest fires are a real and present danger here – especially in eucalyptus forests. One cigarette can cause decades of damage.

DON'T SAY "GRACIAS"
You may well be proud of the Spanish you can speak but don't forget Portugal was occupied by Spain for a long time so, although most people in Portugal understand Spanish, it can be considered rude if you speak it. "Obrigada" is just as easy to say as "gracias".

DO WALK, DON'T DRIVE IN TOWNS
When building the old towns in Portugal, no one ever imagined the advent of cars and the streets are proof of this. They get easily blocked and town-centre driving can be very stressful. Find a car park on the outskirts and walk if you can.

DO CHECK THE PRICE OF FISH
Fish and seafood are often sold by the kilogram in restaurants. If you get it wrong when ordering, you may be faced with an unexpectedly big bill. Ask the staff to weigh things before ordering so that you are spared any nasty surprises.